The New York Review
QUIZ BOOK

The New York Review

QUIZ BOOK

BY THE NEW YORK REVIEW OF BOOKS

DRAWINGS BY EDWARD GOREY

CROWN PUBLISHERS, INC. NEW YORK

Permissions appear on page 169

Published by Crown Publishers, Inc., 225 Park Av-
enue South, New York, New York, 10003 and rep-
resented in Canada by the Canadian MANDA Group.
CROWN is a trademark of Crown Publishers, Inc.
Manufactured in the United States of America
Library of Congress Cataloging-in-Publication Data
The New York review quiz book.
    1. Literature—Miscellanea.   I. New York re-
view of books.
PN43.N48   1986   802   86-6288
ISBN 0-517-55987-0
10 9 8 7 6 5 4 3 2 1
First Edition

Introduction

Someone once berated James Joyce, in the years when he was writing *Finnegans Wake*, for squandering his gifts on mere wordplay. As a former pupil of the Jesuits, Joyce was well acquainted with the doctrines of the medieval Schoolmen, who divided the liberal arts into two branches—the trivium or threefold way to eloquence (grammar, rhetoric, and logic) and the quadrivium or fourfold way to knowledge (arithmetic, music, geometry, and astronomy). So when he was asked whether his puns and verbal puzzles weren't essentially trivial, he was able to reply in a flash, "Yes, of course—and quadrivial too."

While it might be too much to claim that *The New York Review Quiz Book* represents an example of quadrivial pursuit, the quizzes in it *are* meant to have an extra dimension. They are tests of ingenuity as well as knowledge; many of the questions contain hidden clues, for example, and there are often subterranean links between one part of a question and another.

It is only fair to add that quite a few of the questions are perfectly straightforward, without frills or elaborations. In some cases it should be obvious which these are; in other cases, rather less obvious.

For anyone worried about not getting a high score, it ought to be pointed out that the quizzes are intended to be tricky even by the loftiest standards. We hope, too, that the answers will be no less intriguing even if in the end you have to look them up.

To those who continue to object that quizzes are unworthy of anyone with a serious interest in literature, we can only point out that it was a great and intensely serious writer who took as his motto, "Vive la bagatelle!"—"Long live mere frivolities!" Who was he, incidentally? His name (all five letters of it) can be found concealed in this introduction—for openers, as it were.

The
QUESTIONS

Answers start on page 91.

To start with, some (more or less) straightforward questions about titles. Who wrote the following?

a. *We*
b. *She*
c. *"They"*
d. *One of Ours*
e. *Not I*
f. *Ego*
g. *Ich und Du*
h. *Elle et Lui*

3

2

a. *To the North*
b. *North and South*
c. *South*
d. *Eastward Hoe*
e. *Westward Ha!*
f. *Worstward Ho*

3.

a. *Northwest Passage*
b. *A Rhetoric of Motives*
c. *Curtains*
d. *Memoirs of a Shy Pornographer*
e. *The Big Clock*
f. *The Peculiar Institution*
g. *Thank You and Other Poems*

4.

a. *Love and Friendship*
b. *Love and Freindship*

5.

a. *L'Ami Commun*
b. *Le Cher Disparu*
c. *La Veille des Rois*
d. *Les Raisins de la Colère*
e. *La Dernière Chemise de l'Amour*

a. *Ruth*

b. *Rebecca*

c. *Naomi*

d. *Esther*

e. the other *Esther*

a. *Albinos in Black, Lost Property,* and *The Doubtful Asphodel*

b. "Ode to an Expiring Frog"

c. "Oh Hollow! Hollow! Hollow!" (A poem that the author himself described as "a wild, weird, fleshly thing; yet very tender, *very* yearning, very precious.")

a. *An Essay on Woman*

b. *The Women*

c. *Men and Women*

d. *Men Without Women*

e. *An Essay on Man*

a. *The Purple Land*

b. *The Mauve Decade*

c. *Prater Violet*

a. *Green Mansions*
b. *The House with the Green Shutters*
c. *The Greening of America*
d. "Looking for Mr. Green"
e. *Nothing*

What were the original names of the following writers?

a. Henry David Thoreau

b. William Faulkner

c. Bertolt Brecht

What writers have or had the following middle names?

a. Taliaferro

b. Klapka

c. Mallahan

In which poems do the following lines occur?

a. *"L'Académie Groton, eh, c'est une école admirable"*

b.   *J'erre toujours de-ci de-là*
       A divers coups de tra là là
       De Damas jusqu'à Omaha.

Which writer or writers do you associate with

a. Peter Doyle
b. Larry Doyle
c. Dickie Doyle

What is the difference between *Finnegans Wake* and *Howard's End*?

What is the connection between

a. Jennie Gerhardt and "My Gal Sal"
b. Margot Metroland and *Island in the Sun*
c. Clavdia Chauchat and *The Blue Angel*

What eventually happened to *The High-Bouncing Lover* and *Trimalchio in West Egg*?

Some unromantic reflections by a nobleman who committed suicide shortly afterwards. Who was he?

> Byron! He would be all but forgotten today if he had lived to be a florid old gentleman with iron-grey whiskers writing very long, very able letters to "The Times" about the Repeal of the Corn Laws. Yes, Byron would have been that. It was indicated in him. He would have been an old gentleman exacerbated by Queen Victoria's invincible prejudice against him, her brusque refusal to "entertain" Lord John Russell's timid nomination of him for a post in the Government... Shelley would have been a poet to the last. But how dull, how very dull, would have been the poetry of his middle age!—a great unreadable mass interposed between him and us...

Who wrote

a. *His Monkey Wife*

b. *Lady Into Fox*

c. *The Old Men at the Zoo*

And in which novel is an orang-outan elected a member of Parliament?

III **NEW YORK, N.Y.**

What was the principal service performed for literature by Orson and Lorenzo Fowler?

Who received the following invitation?

> *From Brooklyn Bridge, over the Brooklyn Bridge, on*
> *this fine morning,*
>> *please come flying.*
> *In a cloud of fiery pale chemicals*
>> *please come flying,*
> *to the rapid rolling of thousands of small blue drums*
> *descending out of the mackerel sky*
> *over the glittering grandstand of harbor-water,*
>> *please come flying.*

Who maintained that "it'd take a guy a lifetime to know Brooklyn t'roo and t'roo"? "An' even den, you wouldn't know it all."

The unmeasured treasures of Manhattan—who is contemplating them here?

> *Has anyone ever figured out, in hard cash, the value of the objects of art stored upon Manhattan Island? I narrow it to the paintings, and bar out all the good ones. What would it cost to replace even the bad ones? Or all the statuary, bronzes, hangings, pottery and bogus antiques? Or the tons of bangles, chains of pearls, stomachers, necklaces and other baubles? Assemble all the diamonds into one colossal stone, and you will have a weapon to slay Behemoth.*

In which play does the main character meet his death in a cage in the Bronx Zoo?

a. Who—among other things—got a shoeshine because he was going to Easthampton, had a hamburger and a malted, went into the Golden Griffin to get a little Verlaine for Patsy, went into the Park Lane Liquor Store to get a bottle of Strega for Mike, and then bought a copy of the *New York Post* and read some bad news about Billie Holiday?

b. Where could you see autographed caricatures of— among other well-known local figures—Silvana Casamassima, Vic Blad (the talent agent), Max Dove, A. Lincoln Brown, Beryl Cohn (theatrical attorney), Morty Monroe, Sir Jack Handel Bart., Del Hector (the producer), Fab Newcome, and His Honor Judge Perutz?

Which of the following is the odd one out?
42nd Street; Mott Street; *Abie's Irish Rose*; Delancey Street; *My Fair Lady*

"Rings on her fingers and bells on her toes, And she shall cure dandruff wherever she goes." In which novel does a girl ride through midtown Manhattan on a white horse advertising "Danderene"?

a. Who wrote the following? (By way of a clue, he also wrote a novel about a senator.)

> *I have never walked down Fifth Avenue alone without thinking about money. I have never walked there with a companion without thinking of it. I fancy that every man there, in order to maintain the spirit of the place, should bear on his forehead a label stating how many dollars he is worth, and that every label should be expected to assert a falsehood.*

b. Who wrote the following? (By way of a clue, his other writings include a book—not about New York—called *Bloody Murder*.)

> *A walk in Central Park,*
> *New York friends tell me, is far from being a lark.*
> *If lucky enough to escape attack by muggers*
> *You will attract the more insidious attentions of buggers.*

12

c. Who observed, on first seeing the lights of Broadway at night, "What a glorious garden of wonders this would be, to anyone who was lucky enough to be unable to read"?

What classic work of American fiction has the subtitle, "A Story of Wall Street"?

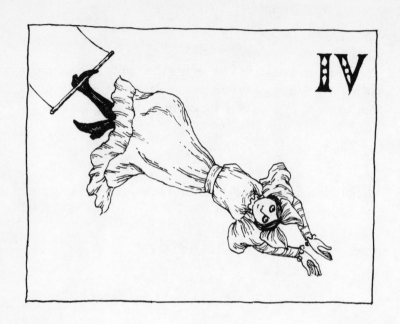

Who wrote the following?

a.   *Women ben full of Ragerie,*
       Yet swinken nat sans Secresie.

b.   *Noontide repayeth never morning-bliss—*
           Sith noon to morn is incomparable;
       And, so it be our dawning goth amiss,
           None other after-hour serveth well.
       Ah! Jesu-Moder, pitie my oe paine—
       Dayspring mishandled cometh not againe!

What do the following have in common?
Paul Heyse; Rudolf Eucken; Henrik Pontoppidan;
Johannes V. Jensen; Winston Churchill

14

Who wrote

a. *Mornings in Mexico*

b. *1001 Afternoons in New York*

c. *My Ten Years in a Quandary*

Where is Llareggub and what is the derivation of its name?

What do the following have in common?
So Big; Scarlet Sister Mary; Now in November; Alice Adams; The Old Man and the Sea

Who was known as

a. Doctor Mirabilis

b. Doctor Angelicus

c. The Dumb Ox

Which piece of research is being introduced in the following passage?

> *The techniques of this research have been taxonomic, in the sense in which modern biologists employ the term. It was born out of the senior author's long-time experience with a problem in insect taxonomy. The transfer from insect to human material is not illogical, for it has been a transfer of a method that may be applied to the study of any variable population.*

What do the following have in common?
William Wordsworth; William Whitehead; Alfred Tennyson; Alfred Austin; Henry James Pye

Who wrote the following poems?

a. "Landscape Near Parma"; "The Double Vortex"; "Rilke and Buddha"

b. "I Remember You"; "Love is my Creed"; "Poem for J."

A parting message—from whom?

> *When by sips of champagne and a few oysters they can no longer keep me from fading away into the infinite azure, "you cannot," I shall whisper my faint last message to the world, "be too fastidious."*

V

Who wrote

a. *The Painted Veil*

b. *Painted Veils*

2

Who are the unfortunate people in the following passage?
What exactly are they up to?

> *Veering through rapids in a vapid rapido*
> *To view the new moon from a ruin on the Lido,*
>
> *Or a sundown in London from a rundown Mercedes,*
> *Then high-borne to Glyndebourne for Orféo in Hades,*

Embarrassed in Paris in Harris tweed, dying to
Get to the next museum piece that they're flying to,

Finding, in Frankfurt, that one indigestible
Comestible makes them too ill for the festival . . .

Who wrote

a. *Main Currents in American Thought*

b. "Main Currents of American Thought"

Who married

a. Charlotte Payne-Townsend

b. Vivien Haigh-Wood

c. Georgie Hyde-Lees

What does *World Enough and Time* by Robert Penn Warren have in common with *Beyond the Mexique Bay* by Aldous Huxley?

Who married Emma Rouault?

a. Who had an aunt called Dante?

b. Whose schemes included the distribution of immaculate contraceptives for the populace and mare's milk for the sick?

c.   *For everyone knows the Pope can't belch*
      Without the permission of—
Who?

18

Who wrote the following poems or collections of verse?

a. *The Spanish Gypsy*

b. *Deaths for the Ladies*

c. *Hoping for a Hoopoe*

d. *The True-Born Englishman*

e. *Babbling April*

a. Who is reputed to have exclaimed, and of which work, "My God! the hero's a bee!"

b. Who was reluctantly persuaded to keep which biblical figure out of the Wars of the Roses?

c. Who was reputed to have a very large family and also had his biography written by the English poet John Drinkwater?

Who wrote

a. *On the Harmful Effects of Tobacco*

b. *My Lady Nicotine*

c. *Smoke*

VI
FOOD
AND DRINK

Room! room! make room for the bouncing Belly,
First father of sauce and deviser of jelly...

The opening lines of "A Hymn to the Belly." Who wrote it?

a. Which character in which novel thought that "an egg, boiled soft, is not unwholesome"?

b. Which poem contains repeated references to butter, eggs, and cheese?

c. "Oh no, my Lord, I assure you! Parts of it are excellent!" Parts of what?

d. Who went on cutting bread and butter?

Where can you find the following comments?

a. Oysters: Nobody eats them any more; too expensive.

b. Mustard: Good only in Dijon. Ruins the stomach.

c. Champagne: The sign of a ceremonial dinner. Pretend to despise it, saying "It's really not a wine."

a. Who wrote to his sister:

> I should like now to promenade round your Garden— apple-tasting—pear-tasting—plum-judging—apricot- nibbling— peach-scrunching—nectarine sucking and melon-carving. I also have a great feeling for anti- quated cherries full of sugar cracks...

b. And who complained to his hostess, "Toujours straw- berries and cream"?

Where is "an aged and a great wine" the subject of the following exchange?

> "Another bottle is to follow."
> "No!"
> "It is ordered."
> "I protest."
> "It is uncorked."
> "I entreat."
> "It is decanted."
> "I submit."

21

Chum Frink wrote the following reflections for the benefit of his fellow citizens. Shortly afterward he went to a cocktail party. In which city did he live?

> I sate alone and groused and thunk and scratched my head and sighed and wunk, and groaned, "There still are boobs, alack, who'd like the old-time gin-mill back; that den that makes the sage a loon, the vile and smelly old saloon!" I'll never miss their poison booze, whilst I the bubbling spring can use, that leaves my head at merry morn as clear as any babe new-born!

> They put arsenic in his meat
> And stood aghast to watch him eat;
> They poured strychnine in his cup
> And shook to see him drink it up.

Who survived this unpromising course of treatment?

Which novel contains recipes for sorrel soup, bacon hash, peach pie, Swiss potatoes, and a method of making four-minute eggs in three minutes?

Which heroine is being subjected to the following ordeal?

> "A chili," said R——gasping, "Oh yes!" She thought a chili was something cool, as its name imported, and was served with some. "How fresh and green they look!" she said, and put one into her mouth. It was hotter than the curry; flesh and blood could bear it

no longer. *"Water, for Heaven's sake water!"* she cried. Mr. S——burst out laughing *(he was a coarse man, from the Stock Exchange, where they love all sorts of practical jokes).*

Complete the following couplet:
Serenely full, the epicure would say...

First Crossword

Solution on page 109

Across

1. A metropolitan march-past? Possibly (3, 4, 6)

9. According to Auden this sailor "wore a stammer like a deco-ration" (5, 4)

10. I could be in the same spot as St. Columba, or a Europeanized region of Asia (5)

11. Conspirator said to be responsible for rent (5)

12. Author and man of action in the air force (4)

13. It's a backward product of Piedmont (4)

15. Asked for spare change during the Depression (5)

16. Keats said that Wordsworth was one, to a sublime degree (7)

17. Muddled again, the sun god falls (7)

19. Country bumpkins depicted the lion lying down with the lamb (5)

20. Busy—the first part of his first name (4)

21. Donatello resembled one (4)

22. A change of girth sounds no more than your due (5)

25. Lord, he defined the effects of power (5)

26. Urge on a soldier lying back in state if you get in first (9)

27. A philosopher rebuilt ego as a strategy (6, 1, 6)

Down

1. Portrayed by Blake on all fours (14)

2. Cymru (5)

3. He once spread despair in an antique land (10)

4. Karl the Marxist (7)

5. The harrowing of Hamm (7)

6. Endlessly Hibernian—associated with the bell, the sandcastle, and the rainbow (4)

7. An integument surrounded by alcoholic beverages—or the reverse (9)

8. Out of doors but not out of the ordinary (3, 2, 3, 6)

14. Once a cretin, if you forgot the East, could be shaken up, producing music (10)

15. Senator who was roused up against his son-in-law (9)

18. Meredith's marriage (7)

19. The senator's son-in-law misjudged this quality (7)

23. The senator's son-in-law thought of these in connection with monkeys (5)

24. Shaw's was irrational (4)

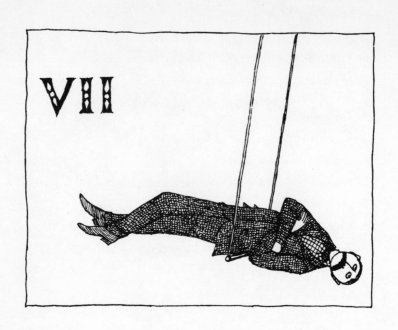

Who wrote the following?

a.　　*Thou knowst how heappily they Freind*
　　　　Walks upon florid Ways;
　　　Thou knowst how heavens bounteous hand
　　　　Leads him to golden days.

　　　But hah! a cruel ennemy
　　　　Destroies all that Bless;
　　　In moments of Melancholy
　　　　Flies all my Happiness.

b.   *Si ta fraîcheur nous étonne tant,*
     heureuse rose,
     c'est qu'en toi-même, en dedans,
     pétale contre pétale, tu te reposes.

     Ensemble tout éveillé, dont le milieu
     dort, pendant qu'innombrables, se touchent
     les tendresses de ce coeur silencieux
     qui aboutissent a l'extrême bouche.

What do truth-loving Persians never dwell upon?

Which of the following is the odd one out?
Blenholt; Provence; Catalonia; Daniel Shays

Who found harlots cheaper than hotels?

What is the nominal connection between *Kim* and *Gone
With the Wind*? And what, if anything, does this question
have to do with the previous one?

"Three-fifths of him genius, and two-fifths sheer fudge."
Who?

Whose boyhood memories, as recalled in their autobiographical accounts, are these?

a. *I had scarcely passed my twelfth birthday when I entered the inhospitable region of examinations, through which for the next seven years I was destined to journey. These examinations were a great trial to me. The subjects which were dearest to the examiners were almost invariably those I fancied least. I would have liked to have been examined in history, poetry and writing essays. The examiners, on the other hand, were partial to Latin and mathematics. But their will prevailed . . .*

b. *For the first time in my life—I was then eleven years old—I felt myself forced into open opposition. No matter how hard and determined my father might be about putting his own plans and opinions into action, his son was no less obstinate in refusing to accept ideas on which he set little or no value.*

   I would not become a civil servant.

Who is burning in Hell for his hand-maimed host?

What is wrong with the following titles?

a. *Yours Sincerely, Thomas Harrow*

b. *Youngblood Royal*

c. *The Rise of Silas Levinsky*

What, in reality, became of Waring?

VIII

In which works are the following characters to be found?

a. Peter Quilpe

b. Peter Quint

c. Peter Quince

a. Who wrote an encyclopaedia of sex and was subsequently sentenced to death?

b. Who wrote a history of the cinema (together with a colleague) and was subsequently sentenced to death?

c. Who wrote a history of the world and was also sentenced to death?

Of which countries are the following the capital cities?

a. Amaurote

b. Mildendo

c. Strelsau

a. Who said of which poet that he *"walks* as if he had fouled his small-clothes, and *looks* as if he smelt it?"

b. Who said of which poet that he was shunned for "not loving clean linen"? (The speaker added that he had "no passion for it" himself.)

What happened one day in a prominent bar in Secaucus?

Who wrote

a. *Venus Observed*

b. *Venus in Furs*

c. *One Touch of Venus*

Arrange the following names in pairs:
Hall; Hitchcock; Bentley; Liveright; Reynal; Gwyer; Chapman; Colburn; Boni; Faber

Who wrote the following?
Man has been here 32,000 years. That it took a

hundred million years to prepare the world for him is proof that that is what it was done for. I suppose it is. I dunno. If the Eiffel Tower were now representing the world's age, the skin of paint on the pinnacle-knob at its summit would represent man's share of that age; and anybody would perceive that that skin was what the tower was built for. I reckon they would. I dunno.

With which book are the following names connected? Breeches, Vinegar, Moffat, Coverdale, Geneva

"En la komenco Dio kreis la ĉielon kaj la teron." No prizes for guessing what this is a translation of—but into which language has it been translated?

IX CRIMINAL RECORDS

a. It turned out that Archer had been killed by O'Shaughnessy. What were their first names? And what were the last names of Caspar and Joel?

b. What was the name of the person hired to solve a murder in Personville?

a. Who wrote a story based on the murder of Mary Cecilia Rogers?

b. Who wrote a novel based on a murder committed by Chester Gillette?

If the orange was Chinese, what were the cape, the shoe, and the hat?

Who created the following detectives?

a. Tecumseh Fox

b. Parker Pyne

c. Bertha Cool

He wrote a detective story about the murder of a financier called Sigsbee Manderson; a friend and former school-mate dedicated a thriller about anarchists to him (the dedication took the form of a poem); the friend was closely associated with another writer, whose sister wrote a novel based on the Jack the Ripper killings. What were the titles of the three books in question?

Which of the following is the odd one out?
Bert Kling; Matthew Hope; Cotton Hawes; Eddie Mars; Meyer Meyer

Who was proposed to in Latin by the younger brother of the Duke of Denver, replied to him in Latin, and married him?

Who wrote the following?

a. "The Guilty Vicarage"

b. "The Simple Art of Murder"

c. "Murder Considered as One of the Fine Arts"

d. "On the Distinction between the Ashes of the Various Tobaccos"

e. "Mr. Holmes, They Were the Footsteps of a Gigantic Hound!"

Distinguish between Gervase Fen and Gideon Fell

In which novel does the following passage occur?

> She had not heard my entrance into the room; and I allowed myself the luxury of admiring her for a few moments, before I moved one of the chairs near me, as the least embarrassing means of attracting her attention. She turned towards me immediately. The easy elegance of every movement of her limbs and body as soon as she began to advance from the far end of the room, set me in a flutter of expectation to see her face clearly. She left the window—and I said to myself, The lady is dark. She moved forward a few steps—and I said to myself, The lady is young. She approached nearer—and I said to myself (with a sense of surprise which words fail me to express), The lady is ugly!

Rilke once worked for her lover; Dylan Thomas had his portrait painted by her brother. Who was she?

a. Which American author killed his wife while trying to shoot a glass off her head?

b. Which American author jumped off a ship crying "Goodbye, everybody!"?

c. Which American author died as a result of swallowing a toothpick while eating an hors d'oeuvre at a cocktail party?

Which of the following is the odd one out?
Bernard, Susan, Rhoda, Neville, Jinny, Clarissa, Louis

Who wrote the following?

a.   *Surely no spirit or sense of a soul that was soft to the*
      spirit and soul of our senses
   Sweetens the stress of surprising suspicion that sobs
      in the semblance and sound of a sigh;
   Only this oracle opens Olympian in mystical moods
      and triangular tenses—
   "Life is the lust of a lamp for the light that is dark
      till the dawn of the day when we die."

b.   *One, who is not, we see; but one, whom we see not,*
      is:
   Surely this is not that; but that is assuredly this.

Who cried "Let Einstein be!"?

"Oh, Diamond, Diamond, thou little knowest the damage thou hast done!" Who or what was Diamond?

In which poems do the following lines occur?

a.   *John Richard William Alexander Dwyer*

b.   *Xerxes, Ximenes, Xanthus, Xavier?*

c.   *Benjamin Harrison*

"With God he has very suspicious relations; they sometimes remind me of the relations of 'two bears in one den.'" From an account (by a younger writer) of a novelist in his old age—which one?

He had a friend called Kot and a dog called Bibbles and this is his first recorded poem, written when he was about eleven:

> We sit in a lovely meadow
> My sweetheart and me
> And we are oh so happy
> Mid the flowers, birds, and the bees.

Who was he?

Who wrote

a. *The Black Tulip*
b. *The Blue Dahlia*
c. *The Green Carnation*

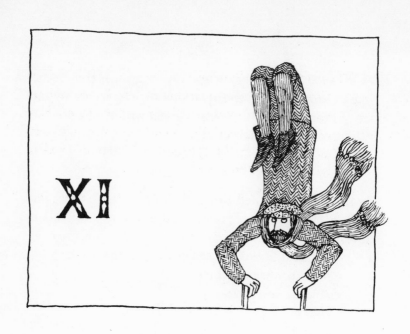

Who wrote to his brother saying that "if I had a prayer to make for any great good, it should be that one of your children should be the first American Poet"

Under what names are the following better known?

a. Beatrice Potter

b. Mary Augusta Arnold

c. Edith Jones

3.

a. Who wrote the following:

> *When I am playing with my cat, who knows whether*
> *she have more sport in dallying with me than I have*
> *in gaming with her? We entertain one another with*
> *mutual apish tricks: if I have my hour to begin or*
> *refuse, so hath she hers.*

b. In which work did Tom and Jerry make their first appearance?

c. What happened to Selima?

d. Who is known in Italy as Topolino?

e. Who wrote a collection of poems entitled *Mice*?

4.

> *You must stir it and stump it,*
> *And blow your own trumpet,*
> *Or, trust me, you haven't a chance.*

Haven't a chance of what?

5.

Who wrote the following epitaphs for themselves?

a. *I am buried by this dyke*
    That my friends might weep as much as they like.

b. *Finis*
    Maginnis

c. *Life is a jest, and all things show it:*
    I thought so once, but now I know it.

Which authors are particularly associated with the following translators?

a. H. T. Lowe-Porter

b. A. A. Brill

c. Willa and Edwin Muir

Who translated *The Enfranchisement of Women* by John Stuart Mill into German?

a. For which work is Lord Berners best known as a translator?

b. Who wrote the words for Lord Berners' choral ballet *A Wedding Bouquet*?

Who wrote the following?

> The colonel's subjects were sheep (in sickness and in health), manure, wheat, mangold-wurzels, huntin', shootin' and fishin': while Sacheverell was at his best on Proust, the Russian ballet, Japanese prints, and the influence of James Joyce on the younger Bloomsbury novelists. There was no fusion between these

men's souls. Colonel Branksome did not actually bite Sacheverell in the leg, but when you have said that you have said everything.

What disappeared "with a curious Perfume and a most melodious Twang"?

XII
ON STAGE

---

a. What did Poquelin and Coquelin have in common?

b. Who was John Henry Brodribb?

c. What does Laurence Olivier have in common with David Garrick—apart from a certain amount of theatrical experience, that is?

d. Her aunt was painted by Reynolds, Gainsborough, and Lawrence; one of her grandson's novels was made into a movie with Gary Cooper. Who was she?

e. He broke both legs working as a circus acrobat, and Jean-Paul Sartre wrote a play about him. Who was he?

Who wrote the following plays?

a. *Irene*

b. *Remorse*

c. *The High Bid*

a. In which play is there a mayor of Chicago called Dogsborough?

b. In which play is there a cabaret performer called Destructive Desmond who hacks a Rembrandt to pieces?

c. In which play is a dog put on trial for stealing cheese?

d. What do Nan and Sheba have in common?

In which play does the playwright who wrote *The Heiress* himself appear as a character?

a. What do the initials R.U.R. stand for?

b. In which play is there a character called Shrdlu?

a. What was used by Charles I (quite informally) and later by George IV (on a journey north)?

b. Which ghost had a nominal connection with Don Juan and a titular connection with Shelley's "Ode to the West Wind"?

c. To whom did two visitors to Iceland bequeath a place in the setting sun?

a. He was the editor of the British magazine *Punch*, but it is his work as a playwright that has won him a place in American history. Who was he?

b. He wrote a poem about Brooklyn Bridge and a play about a man who is accidentally frozen in a block of ice and brought to life again in the year 1978. Who was he?

c. He began life working for a pharmacist; the hero of one of his best-known plays earns his living retouching photographs. Who was he?

Who wrote a play called *The Spanish Armada*?

a. Who left an astrakhan coat at Willis's and another one at the Savoy?

b. What was the relationship between Speranza and C.3.3?

What is the connection between the following?

a. John Hall and Thomas Quiney

b. Sigmund Freud and Thomas Looney

c. Robin Goodfellow and Mickey Rooney

Who wrote the following lines?

a.   *His nose was as sharp as any pen, and 'a babbled of green fields.*

b.   *No light, but rather a transpicuous gloom.*

What is the connection between Sir Joshua Mattheson and Mr. Apollinax?

With which writers are the following places associated?

a. Olney
b. Sirmione
c. Vailima
d. Guernsey
e. Ferney

Which of the following is the odd one out?

Puffs, patches, powders, brooches, Bibles, billets-doux

Who wrote

a. *Puzzled Americans*
b. *An American Dilemma*
c. *Say! Is This the U.S.A.?*

a. Where do the early pumpkins blow?
b. Whose grandmother threatened to burn her?
c. Who reads (though he cannot speak) Spanish?

What is the connection between *The Turn of the Screw*, "Land of Hope and Glory," Lucia and the religious beliefs of Ronald Firbank?

In which novel does the following deathbed scene occur?

His mind ran rather upon his career, and usually, I am glad to recall, with a note of satisfaction and approval. In his delirious phases he would most often exaggerate this self-satisfaction, and talk of his splendours. He would pluck at the sheet and stare before him, and whisper half-audible fragments of sentences.

"What is this great place, these cloud-capped towers, these airy pinnacles? . . . Ilion. Sky-y-pointing . . . Ilion House, the residence of one of our great merchant princess . . . Terrace above terrace. Reaching to the Heavens . . . Kingdoms Caesar never knew . . . A great poet, George. Zzzz. Kingdoms Caesar never knew . . . Under entirely new management.

"Greatness . . . Millions . . . Universities . . . He stands on the terrace—on the upper terrace—directing—directing—by the globe—directing—the trade . . ."

a. Who were the authors of *The Real Charlotte*?

b. Who were the authors of *The Male Animal*?

c. Who were the authors of *The Custom of the Country*?

Complete the following couplets:

a.   *The cat, the rat, and Lovell the dog*

b.   *I am his Highness' dog at Kew—*

Second Crossword

Solution on page 133

The completed crossword grid reads:

Row 1: S T O I C / T I R E S I A S
Row 2: E D O H / R N E
Row 3: L A D Y A N N E / F I E S T A
Row 4: S S F S / K T S
Row 5: R O U S S E A U / P S M I T H
Row 6: N E S N / O N E
Row 7: A / U N S H A V E N / C
Row 8: E L M S / O L N / E T A L
Row 9: N E / T R I S T R A M / L
Row 10: O R H / O O E / G
Row 11: R O C K E L / R E P O R T E R
Row 12: M H R / I E I R
Row 13: O C A S E Y / S M A R T I N G
Row 14: U A S / E N U O
Row 15: S I T W E L L S / S U S A N

Across

1. Following Zeno, or following a financier and a titan (5)

4. Blind and bisexual—satire is confounded (8)

8. She married a monster in spite of herself (4, 4)

9. 4d. calls for celebration in Britain (6)

10. Solitary stroller who started out in Switzerland (8)

11. Wodehouse character starts out with an afterthought (6)

12. Frequently applicable to Brecht, and us, as he might have said—leading into harbor (8)

14. They overshadowed a passionate entanglement in New England (4)

15. An extraterrestrial, a gangster, and other things (2, 2)

18. Tragically involved with his uncle Mark or comically involved with his uncle Toby (8)

19. What you should do with a cradle, by the sound of it, or a missile (6)   *Rocket*

20. Correspondent makes pet error (8)

21. Red roses for him (6)

22. Fashionable gin cocktail has painful results (8)

23. Rebels from Renishaw (8)

24. Lady whom Jane Austen wrote about (5)

Down

1. Thomson's thoughts frequently were (8)

2. Man of many devices (8)

3. 10a.—led the way in Westminster Abbey (9)

4. Osla nus eht (3, 3, 4, 5)

5. He has analyzed moments of truth in Wittenberg and Amritsar (7)

6. In a street in Connecticut, it comes naturally (8)

7. Tongue-twisting mollusk when it's for sale (8)

13. Felix and Eugenia from a New England point of view (9)

14. A poet's room was, when he wrote prose (8)

15. Poetically, he was preoccupied with what took place between January and May; dramatically, his title is often taken to refer to his antagonist (8)

16. In cases of mal de mer it usually signifies honorable retirement (8)

17. Preceding Sidney, a republican; followed in the first instance by Charles, a singer before sunrise (8)

18. Raquin or Desqueyroux (7)

XIV

Who was or were MacSpaunday?

a. Who wrote a novel in which the central character is based on Ferdinand Lassalle?

b. Who wrote "Where Engels Fears to Tread"?

c. What does Karl Marx have in common with George Eliot and Radclyffe Hall?

Who is venting his (or her) indignation in this account of the kind of men who take advantage of women?

> *They are snakes in the grass who do not place woman upon a pedestal. They are cads who kiss and tell, who*

trifle with a girl's affections and betray her innocent trust. They are cynics who think that a woman is only a woman, but a good cigar is a smoke. Their mottoes are "Love 'em and leave 'em" and "Catch 'em young, treat 'em rough, tell 'em nothing." These cads speak of "the light that lies in a woman's eyes, and lies—and lies—and lies"... They are fiends in human form, and would rob a woman of her most priceless possession.

Which of the following is the odd one out?
Cheap red wine; amethysts; emeralds; diamonds; cheap tin trays

Who was in love with

a. Tomasso Cavalieri

b. Angelo Fusato

c. Alfred Agostinelli

What was the occasion of the following replies or retorts?

a. If you were a mere gentleman, I should not have come to see you.

b. Ignorance, Madam, pure ignorance.

c. Regret... Remorse... RELIEF...

And to what was this a riposte?

His son's a Jew—
I thought you knew.

What do the following words or phrases have in common? hotdog; yes-man; the once-over; see what the boys in the backroom will have; for crying out loud

Who wrote this?

> Often I used to see, after painting upon the blank darkness a sort of rehearsal while waiting, a crowd of ladies, and perhaps a festival and dances. And I heard it said or I said to myself, "These are English ladies from the unhappy times of Charles I. These are the wives and daughters of those who met in peace, and sat at the same tables, and were allied by marriage, or by blood; and yet, after a certain day in August 1642, never smiled upon each other again nor met but in the field of battle; and at Marston Moor, at Newbury, or at Naseby, cut asunder all this of love by the cruel sabre, and washed away in blood the memory of ancient friendship." The ladies danced, and looked as lovely as at the court of George IV.

a. Who illustrated *The Rape of the Lock* and wrote *Under the Hill*?

b. Who illustrated poems by Tennyson and A. E. Housman and wrote *Lanterns and Lances*?

c. Who illustrated poems by Stevie Smith and wrote *Novel on Yellow Paper*?

Pictorial Quiz

Of which famous works are the illustrations on this and the following pages, and who were the illustrators?

Answers start on page 137

XV

BRUSH AND PALETTE

*When they talked of their Raphaels, Correggios and
        stuff,*
He shifted his trumpet and only took snuff.

Who was he?

a. Who wrote *Desire Caught by the Tail?*

b. Which artists do you associate with *The Man with the
Blue Guitar?*

3.

a. Who wrote the following?
        There's a combative artist named Whistler
        Who is, like his own hog's-hairs, a bristler:
        A tube of white lead
        And a punch on the head
        Offer varied attractions to Whistler.

b. Who told Whistler that he behaved as though he didn't have any talent?

c. Who was Joe Sibley?

Which writer do you connect with the artists Martin Droeshout and Giulio Romano?

Which artist, according to whom,

> . . . had a quaint
> Way of saying to his sibyl
> "Shall I dribble?
> Shall I paint?"
> And with never an instant's quibble
> Sibyl always answered,
> "Dribble."

In which works can the following painters be found?

a. Hans Meyrick

b. Lily Briscoe

c. Louis Dubedat

d. Horace Isbister

e. Charles Strickland

What is being described here, and by whom?

> One who was drinking has left the glass in its position and turned his head towards the speaker. Another, twisting the fingers of his hands together, turns with stern brows to his companion. Another, with hands

spread open and showing the palms, shrugs his shoulders up to his ears, and makes a mouth of astonishment. Another speaks into his neighbour's ear, and he who listens to him turns towards him and lends an ear, holding a knife in one hand, and in the other the bread half cut through the knife. Another in turning, holding a knife in his hand, upsets with his hand a glass over the table. Another lays his hand on the table and is looking. Another breathes hard from full mouth. Another leans forward to see the speaker, shading his eyes with his hand. Another draws back behind the one who leans forward, and sees the speaker between the wall and the man who is speaking.

Who wrote

a. "The Beldonald Holbein"

b. "Du Daumier-Smith's Blue Period"

c. "The Gioconda Smile"

What do the following have in common?

a. *Rumor and Reflection; Praeterita; Another Part of the Wood*

b. *A Little Yes and a Big No; Noa Noa; A Free House*

When he died
        All Nature was degraded;
        The King dropped a tear into the Queen's ear,
        And all his pictures faded.

Who was he?

When a young man who had recently returned home from Paris recalled that he owed some money to G. W. Russell, who might have summed it up as black, white, red, green, and blue?

Who wrote

a. "The Night Before the Night Before Christmas"

b. *In the Heart of the Heart of the Country*

An extract from a diary. Whose? And who was he sitting between? (The two names have been omitted.)

> *I felt stupid between the two wittiest men in Europe, drenched in a Niagara of epigrams. ——— is a stylist and his conversation is full of fire and rapier thrusts . . . He is haggard at 26, and his figure and smile have something mythological, something of the centaur in them.*
>
> *——— is quieter, longer-winded and more meticulous. His blood-shot eyes shine feverishly, as he pours out ceaseless spite and venom about the great. His foibles are Ruskin, genealogy and heraldry. His black hair was tidily arranged, but his linen was grubby, and the rich studs and links had been clumsily put in by dirty fingers.*

What turned out to be

a. A bar of mottled soap

b. A hippopotamus

c. The Middle of Next Week

Which "partial, prejudiced and ignorant historian" wrote the following account of the reign of Henry V?

> *This prince after he succeeded to the throne grew quite reformed & Amiable, forsaking all his dissipated Companions & never thrashing Sir William again. During his reign Lord Cobham was burned alive, but I forget what for. His Majesty then turned his thoughts*

to France, where he went & fought the famous Battle of Agincourt. He afterwards married the King's daughter Catherine, a very agreeable woman by Shakespear's account. In spite of all this however he died, & was succeeded by his son Henry.

By what titles are the following works known in English?

a. *Koheleth*

b. *Nos*

c. *La Carne, La Morte e Il Diavolo nella Letteratura Romantica*

Who didn't Thomas Brown love—and why?

a. Who, apart from Milton, wrote *Paradise Lost*?

b. And who else?

Who were Buzz Windrip, Chuck Crawford, and Willie Stark?

> *Dauntless the slug-horn to my lips I set*
> *And blew, "Childe Roland to the Dark Tower came."*

What exactly is a slug-horn?

Who gife a barty?

Where can the following poems or fragments of verse be found?

a.   *Christ-like in my behaviour,*
      Like every good believer,
      I imitate the Saviour
      And cultivate a beaver.

b. Look down, Conquistador!
    There on the valley's broad green floor,
    There lies the lake; the jewelled cities gleam;
    Chalco and Tlacopan
    Await the coming Man . . .

c. What's he to Hecuba?
    Nothing at all.
    That's why there'll be no wedding on Wednesday
        week,
    Way down in old Bengal.

Who was said to have studied at Oggsford?

What is the source of the following story?

A physician eighty years of age had enjoied of a health unalterable. Their friends did him of it compliment every days. "Mister doctor," they said to him, "you are admirable man. What you are then for to bear you as well?" "I will tell you it, gentlemen," he was answered them; "and I exhort you in same time at to follow my example. I live of the product of my ordering, without any remedy who I command to my sicks."

Who wrote the following?

a. My Sister Eileen

b. Your Daughter, Iris

c. My Cousin Rachel

With which publications are the following lines associated?

a. *Judex damnatur cum nocens absolvitur*—"The judge is condemned when the criminal is acquitted" (Maxims of Publius Syrius)

b. *'Tis the white stag Fame we're hunting, bid the world's hounds come to horn* (Ezra Pound, "The White Stag")

City lights—supply the missing place-names in the following couplets:

    Nebuchadnezzar had it so good?
    wink the lights of ———

    I never think, I have so many things,
    flash the lights of ———

    I cannot quite focus
    cry the lights of ———

    I am a maid of shots & pills
    swivel the lights of ———

What did Margaret Fuller, Moncure Conway, and Scofield Thayer have in common as editors?

Arrange the following persons in three appropriate pairs: A historian of the Risorgimento; an emasculated news-

paperman; two cultured and idealistic sisters who became
involved with a widower called Wilcox; a clergyman who
wrote poetry in a rural dialect; two brothers who were
romantic critics and men of letters; a man who knew he
was right

Who said of his own system "dat only von mans knew
vot der tyfel id meant—und *he* couldn't tell"?

XVIII

CHILDREN'S HOUR

Who turned out to be a balloonist from Nebraska—and a humbug?

Which monarch married his cousin Celeste?

a. Who ate some lettuces and some French beans; and then ate some radishes; and then, feeling rather sick, went to look for some parsley?

b. Who ate a picnic consisting of "coldtonguecoldham-coldbeef pickledgherkin saladfrenchrollscress sandwiches pottedmeatgingerbeerlemonadesodawater"?

Who married an elderly German professor called Mr. Bhaer?

*Not brighter was his eye, nor moister
Than a too-long-opened oyster,
Save when at noon his paunch grew mutinous
For a plate of turtle green and glutinous...*

Whose eye?

Who created

a. A rat called Templeton

b. An opera singer called Madam Castafiore

c. A family called the Bastables

Under what names are the following better known?

a. Theodor Geisel

b. Siegmund Salzmann

c. Cedric Errol

Who wrote the following?

a. *Hector Protector*

b. *Millions of Cats*

c. *The Phantom Tollbooth*

a. Which children's classic was written by a former airline pilot?

b. Which children's author began his literary career with a study of Oscar Wilde, collected Russian legends, and married Trotsky's former secretary?

I⟨O

Who prompted the following comment?

He's had to repeat the history of the race and go through all the stages from the primordial to barbarism. You don't expect boys to be civilized, do you?

XIX

Who wrote the following?

a. *The Stones of Venice*
b. *The Stones of Florence*
c. *The Roman Spring of Mrs. Stone*

What was Amygism?

Supply the missing partners in the following pairs:

a. —— and Grinby

b. Liddell and ——

c. —— and Narcejac

d. Harrigan and ——

e. —— and Crouse

What is the connection between "Daffy Duck in Hollywood," "Houseboat Days," and "Unctuous Platitudes"?

a. When Sir Rufus Isaacs was appointed Lord Chief Justice of England, Kipling wrote a poem about him called "Gehazi." But who wrote about Sir Rufus Israels?

b. What, from a literary point of view, did Charles Ephrussi have in common with Charles Haas?

Who invented the following?

a. Macondo

b. Costaguana

Which family has connections with *The Tempest*, *The Coming Struggle for Power*, *Landmarks in French Literature*, and the writings of Freud?

Who wrote a notable opera based on a play by Ben Jonson—and where and why was it banned?

In which novel can you find the following account of flattery in action?

>"My judgment may not be worth much, Mr. Senator, but it does seem to me that our fathers thought too much of themselves, and till you teach me better I shall continue to think that the passage in your speech of yesterday that began with 'Our strength lies in this twisted and tangled mass of isolated principles, the hair of the half-sleeping giant of Party,' is both for language and imagery quite equal to anything of Webster's."

>The Senator from Illinois rose to this gaudy fly like a huge, two-hundred-pound salmon; his white waistcoat gave out a mild silver reflection as he slowly came to the surface and gorged the hook. He made not even a plunge, not one perceptible effort to tear out the barbed weapon, but floating gently to her feet, allowed himself to be landed as though it were a pleasure.

a. Whose love made him willing to put up with climatic conditions on the coast of Greenland?

b. Who wore fancy gloves and one Sunday morning left a body on the sidewalk bleeding to death?

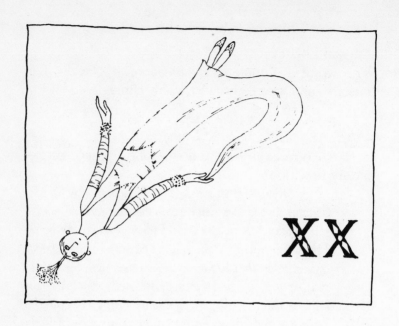

Which famous collection of stories was initiated by Harry Bailly?

Which celebrated novel was made into a movie under the title *We Live Again*?

Distinguish between

a. Anna Seward and Anna Sewell

b. Senlin and Senlac

c. Richard Cory and William Johnson Cory

d. Julian English and William Irish

e. Potterism and One-upmanship

Complete the blanks in the following limerick of the 1920s:

> *I don't like the family ———.*
> *There is ———, there is ———, there is———.*
> *———'s writings are bunk,*
> *———'s statues are junk,*
> *And no one can understand ———.*

a. Who wrote a poem entitled "Verses on the Prospect of Planting Arts and Learning in America"?

b. What did Dr. Proudie have in common with Talleyrand?

c. Who delivered an apology to "Gigadibs, the literary man"?

Complete the following couplet:

> *Who would not give all else for two p*

From the work of which novelist (or, better still, from which novel) does the following passage come?

> *"Oh good gracious me I hope you never kept yourself a bachelor so long on my account . . . but of course you never did why should you, pray don't answer, I*

don't know where I'm running to, oh do tell me something about the Chinese ladies whether their eyes are really so long and narrow always putting me in mind of mother-of-pearl fish at cards and do they really wear tails down their backs and plaited too or is it only the men, and when they pull their hair so very tight off their foreheads don't they hurt themselves, and why do they stick little bells all over their bridges and temples and hats and things or don't they really do it!"

Which of the following is the odd one out?
The Hedgehog and the Fox; *The Lion and the Fox*; *The Lion and the Honeycomb*; *The Mirror and the Lamp*; *The Web and the Rock*

Who wrote the following memoirs or autobiographies?

a. *It Was the Nightingale*

b. *My Host the World*

c. *Blasting and Bombardiering*

d. *Left Hand! Right Hand!*

e. *Inishfallen Fare Thee Well*

What is the family connection between *Daddy Long-Legs* and *Huckleberry Finn*?

XXI
SHAKESPEARE
AND
CO.

Who wrote

a. A short story in which Shakespeare discusses the new King James Bible with Ben Jonson

b. A novel in which Shakespeare contracts syphilis from a prostitute called Lucy Negro

c. A puppet-play in which Shakespeare is knocked out by a right to the jaw

Where could you have heard Othello's jealous doubt spout out or Macbeth raving at a shade-made blade?

Who wrote the following?

> Shakespeare's comedies (exquisite as they certainly
> are), bringing in admirably portrayed common char-
> acters, have the unmistakable hue of plays, portraits,
> made for the divertisement only of the elite of the
> castle, and from its point of view. The comedies are
> altogether non-acceptable to America and Democracy.

a. What did the Mtsensk district have in common with
the Steppes?

b. *The Merry Wives of Windsor* is said to have been written at the request of Queen Elizabeth I. Which European
monarch wrote an adaptation of it under the title *What
It Means to Have a Basket and Linen*?

> I would as lief be thrust into a quickset hedge
> As cry "Plosh" to a callow throstle.

Who successfully claimed that these lines were written
by Shakespeare ("and jolly good Shakespeare they are
too")?

⟨6⟩

What did Wopsle have in common with Sarah Bern-
hardt?

7

Which celebrated letter-writer wrote the following (in
one of his letters)?

> With all my enthusiasm for Shakespeare, The Mer-

chant of Venice *is one of his plays I like the least. The story of the caskets is silly, and, except the character of Shylock, I see nothing beyond the attainment of a mortal; Euripides, or Racine, or Voltaire might have written the rest.*

Who killed her mother, and then went on to help popularize Shakespeare?

In which novel can you find the text of a play by Shakespeare called *The Prince of Antioch, or An Old Way to New Identity,* edited by Miss Blanche Tray? And why does the name Blanche Tray have a Shakespearean ring to it?

Who was originally called Oldcastle?

In which country was a new magazine taken as proof of national sense and national wit?

a. For which of her writings is Katherine Lee Bates best remembered?

b. For which of his writings is Samuel Francis Smith best remembered?

c. Which celebrated words were subsequently set to the music of "Anacreon in Heaven," by the English composer John Stafford Smith?

3.

Who wrote the following?

a.   *But all—with the single exception of Gide*
Who prefers sailor Melville's more masculine breed—
Were exceedingly strong for Henry James,
With his stunningly high artistic aims.
"I've made a discovery! Isn't it thrilling?
He's as good as Stendhal," cried Lionel Trilling.

b.   *. . . Panoplied in*
Virtuous indignation, gnawing his bone,
A man like Leavis plans an Escape.

c.   *I went to see Irving Babbitt*
In the Eighteenth Century clean and neat
When he opened his mouth to speak French
I fell clean off my seat.

4.

What is the connection between the *Aeneid* and *The Chocolate Soldier?*

5.

Who wrote the following?
President Robbins had an M.A. from Oxford—he
had been a Rhodes Scholar—and an LL.D. granted,
in 1947, by Menuire. (It's a college in Florida.) To
make the President dislike you for the rest of his life,
say to him with a resigned anthropological smile: "I've
just been reading that in 1948 Menuire College gave
the degree of Doctor of Humor to Milton Berle."

a. What is this all about?
> *Ter, quater, atque iterum cito vorpalissimus ensis*
> *Snicsnaccans penitus viscera dissecuit*

b. And this?
> *O Freuden-Tag! O Halloo-Schlag!*
> *Er chortelt froh-gesinnt*

Which writer do you associate with the following?

a. Corporal Trim

b. Captain Carpenter

c. Major Molineaux

d. Colonel Brandon

e. General Aupick

a. Whose hair is crisp, and black, and long?

b. Who had ten thousand eyes on him as he rubbed his hands with dirt?

c. What had a general flavor of mild decay?

Who was Lord R'hoone?

Of which novel are these the last lines?
> *Mrs. Tope's care has spread a very neat, clean break-*

fast ready for her lodger. Before sitting down to it, he opens his corner cupboard door; takes his bit of chalk from its shelf; adds one thick line to the score, extending from the top of the cupboard door to the bottom; and then falls to with an appetite.

Third Crossword

Solution on page 165

Across

1. How Nick Dormer's friend might have signed himself in a hurry—a sad grind (5)

4. A poet mixed them up with garlic in the mud (9)

9. A witch's curse, or a cockney friend showing exasperation with 1d. (9)

10. There are few damp skies or dampening words here (5)

11. The city was saved—but now it needs to be saved again (6, 9)

12. Superior location written about by 1d. (6)

14. Have some 24a. (or so it sounds) surrounded by sculpture—those are the rules (8)

17. A novel role, cut short at the beginning and the end and rearranged, leaves you pining (8)

19. A capital storyteller who wrote a book about Eden (6)

22. There was nothing common or mean about his last appearance (7, 3, 5)

24. In a deadly grip, he produces a fine old drink (5)

25. She fell in love while reading about Launcelot (9)

26. Northern neighbor and Southern soldier brought together by an actor (6, 3)

27. "Porter-drinkers' ——— laughter"—Yeats (5)

Down

1. See 9a. and 12a. (4, 5)

2. A.k.a. Hugh Weston (5)

3. She may be victorious when she does or (according to the same writer on another occasion) it may be the death of her (6)

5. They are said to endear absents (8)

6. A poet from Bemerton, or a poet from Lvov (7)

7. What Shaw did to the legend of Androcles (9)

8. The Frank of Frank and Maisie (5)

13. A monster treatise (9)

15. Temple's ruin provides the main subject of this story (9)

16. What Felix Krull, for example, hopes you will be (8)

18. A religious reformer who allegedly mumbled (7)

20. Crouchback was one, and unlike some of the other ones he was also a genuine gentleman (7)

21. A brewer whose widow married an Italian musician—to the consternation of the Great Cham (6)

22. A kind of capacity (5)

23. Reins get tangled—quite sticky (5)

XXIII

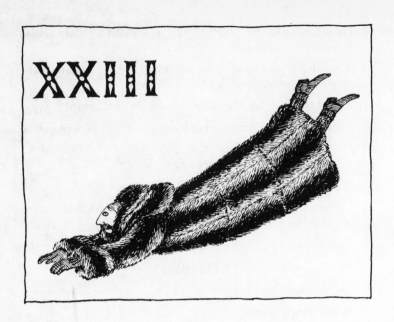

Who wrote the following?

a. *African Game Trails*
b. *Notes on Virginia*
c. *American Individualism*
d. *Crusade in Europe*
e. *A Report on Weights and Measures*

And about whom were the following written?

a. *A Puritan in Babylon*
b. *The Gang's All Here*
c. *Sunrise at Campobello*

3

Summoning artists to participate
In the august occasions of the state
Seems something artists ought to celebrate.

Why was this particular celebration abandoned, and what was the gift that was offered instead?

4

Arrange the following into appropriate pairs: Blofeld, Garfield, Felix Unger, Felix Leiter, Felix Randall, Felix Holt, Felix, Henry Purcell, Oscar Madison, Savonarola

5

His father was a distinguished member of the same profession, his middle name is Meier, he published his first book when he was twenty-one, and he won a major prize when he was twenty-eight. Who is he?

6

Where did Allison MacKenzie cause a furor by writing and publishing a novel?

7

He published a collection of short stories called *Satan in the Suburbs*, he was prevented from teaching in New York, one of his sisters-in-law lived with her husband in Italy, and another one wrote a novel about her life in Prussia. Who was he?

Who wrote the following?

a. *The Rhinemann Exchange*

b. *The Ostermann Weekend*

c. *The Zimmerman Telegram*

Which of the following statements is incorrect?

a. The original of Orlando in Virginia Woolf's novel of that name was Vita Sackville-West, who in private life was Lady Vita Nicolson, the wife of Sir Harold Nicolson

b. The novelist Nathaniel West, whose original name was Nathan Weinstein, was killed in a car crash

c. The poet C. Day-Lewis, who succeeded John Masefield as Poet Laureate, wrote detective stories under the name of "Nicholas Blake"

a. Which writer is said to have drowned while trying to embrace the reflection of the moon in a river?

b. Which writer's last words were "Put out that bloody cigarette!"?

c. Whose last words can roughly be translated as "What an artist the world is losing in me"?

The
ANSWERS

The writer who took as his motto *"Vive la bagatelle!"* was Swift, whose name is spelled out by the first letter in each paragraph of the Introduction.

a. A futuristic novel predicting a totalitarian state by Yevgeni Zamyatin. Published in 1924, it has often been treated as a forerunner of *Brave New World* and *1984*.

b. An adventure story by Sir Henry Rider Haggard

c. A short story by Rudyard Kipling

d. A novel by Willa Cather

e. A brief dramatic monologue by Samuel Beckett

f. The title of a series of autobiographical volumes in the form of diaries by the English theater critic James Agate (1877–1947).

g. A philosophical-cum-theological work by Martin Buber. It is known in English as *I and Thou*.

h. A novel by George Sand based on her love affair with Alfred de Musset

2

a. A novel by Elizabeth Bowen

b. A novel by Mrs. Gaskell, set against an industrial background in early Victorian England; alternatively, a collection of poems by Elizabeth Bishop. There is also a contemporary novel with the same title about the Civil War that has served as the basis of a television series, but it doesn't count.

c. A play about the Civil War by the American-born writer Julian or Julien Green, who writes in French (and who originally wrote it under the title of *Sud*). It is also the title of a collection of stories by the British writer William Sansom, and no doubt various other works.

d. A play by George Chapman, Ben Jonson, and John Marston.

e. S. J. Perelman

f. Once again, Samuel Beckett

3

a. Kenneth Roberts (a novel)

b. Kenneth Burke (a work of literary theory)

c. Kenneth Tynan (a collection of pieces on the theater)

d. Kenneth Patchen (a satirical novel)

e. Kenneth Fearing (a thriller)

f. Kenneth Stampp (a historical study of slavery)

g. Kenneth Koch

4

a. A novel by Alison Lurie

b. A piece of juvenilia by Jane Austen

a. The title under which *Our Mutual Friend* by Charles Dickens was originally published in French

b. The title of the French translation of *The Loved One* by Evelyn Waugh

c. The title of the French translation of Shakespeare's *Twelfth Night*

d. The title of the French translation of *The Grapes of Wrath* by John Steinbeck

e. The title of the eighteenth-century French translation of Colley Cibber's play *Love's Last Shift*—a celebrated example of the translator getting it wrong

a. A novel by—once again—Mrs. Gaskell

b. A novel by Daphne du Maurier

c. A novel by the Japanese writer Junichiro Tanizaki

d. Either the play by Racine or the novel by Henry Adams

e. Vice versa. There is also a seventeenth-century epic called *Esther* by Jean Desmarets de Saint-Sorlin; but if you know about that you are probably wondering why this question doesn't also include the Yiddish novel *Deborah* by Esther Kreitman (Isaac Bashevis Singer's sister), the German play *Judith* by Friedrich Hebbel, the French play *Judith* by Jean Giraudoux, and possibly other biblical or biblically named ladies.

7

a. They are all novels by Sebastian Knight, the central character in Vladimir Nabokov's novel *The Real Life of Sebastian Knight*.

b. A poem by Mrs. Leo Hunter, the lionizing literary hostess in *The Pickwick Papers* by Charles Dickens

c. Reginald Bunthorne, the "fleshly poet" in *Patience* by Gilbert and Sullivan

a. A parody of Pope by the eighteenth-century British politician John Wilkes. After it had been condemned as an obscene libel, he was expelled from Parliament.

b. A play by Clare Boothe Luce

c. A collection of poems by Robert Browning

d. A collection of stories by Ernest Hemingway

e. A poem—*the* poem—by Alexander Pope

a. A collection of stories set in South America by W. H. Hudson

b. A study of the 1890s by Thomas Beer

c. A short novel by Christopher Isherwood

a. A novel by—once again—W. H. Hudson

b. A novel—and a very fine one—by the Scottish author George Douglas, first published in 1901

c. A tract for the times (published in 1970) by Charles Reich

d. A story by Saul Bellow

e. A novel by the British novelist who was born Henry Yorke but wrote under the name Henry Green

a. David Henry Thoreau

b. William Falkner

c. Bertold Brecht (who changed "Bertold" to "Bertolt" to make the name sound harder, in emulation of his friend Arnolt—formerly Arnold—Bronnen)

a. Booker T(aliaferro) Washington

b. Jerome K(lapka) Jerome

c. James M(allahan) Cain

a. "Harvard" by Robert Lowell, from *Notebook*. The speaker is Paul Claudel.

b. "Mélange adultère de tout" by T. S. Eliot

a. Peter Doyle was the young Washington streetcar conductor befriended by Walt Whitman in the 1860s.

b. Larry Doyle is one of the central characters in Bernard Shaw's play *John Bull's Other Island*

c. Richard Doyle, commonly known as Dickie, was one of the foremost early Victorian cartoonists and illustrators (he designed the original cover of *Punch*). Among the books he illustrated were some of Dickens' Christmas stories and *The King of the Golden River* by John Ruskin; he was also the uncle of Arthur Conan Doyle.

5

Finnegans Wake is correctly spelled, without an apostrophe; *Howard's End* is incorrectly spelled, with an apostrophe.

a. Jennie Gerhardt is the heroine of *Sister Jennie* by Theodore Dreiser; "My Gal Sal" is a song by his brother, the songwriter Paul Dresser.

b. Margot Metroland (formerly Margot Beste-Chetwynde) is a character who appears in *Decline and Fall* and subsequent novels by Evelyn Waugh; *Island in the Sun* is a novel (subsequently turned into a well-known movie) by his brother Alec Waugh.

c. Clavdia Chauchat is a character in *The Magic Mountain* by Thomas Mann; the movie *The Blue Angel* was based on the novel *Professor Unrat* by his brother Heinrich Mann.

The two titles were considered and rejected by Scott Fitzgerald for the story that eventually became *The Great Gatsby*.

The Duke of Dorset in *Zuleika Dobson* by Max Beerbohm

a. A novel by John Collier
b. A novel by David Garnett
c. A novel by Angus Wilson

Melincourt by Thomas Love Peacock—he was elected under the name of Sir Oran Haut-Ton. The episode satirizes the views of the pioneer eighteenth-century anthropologist Lord Monboddo, who argued that the higher primates had most of the essential characteristics of human beings apart from speech.

III NEW YORK, N.Y.

Orson and Lorenzo Fowler were phrenologists in nineteenth-century Manhattan. Together with Samuel Wells they ran the phrenological emporium of Fowler and Wells on Broadway, which distributed the first edition of Walt Whitman's *Leaves of Grass* and published the second edition.

The opening lines of "Invitation to Miss Marianne Moore," by Elizabeth Bishop

The speaker in Thomas Wolfe's short story "Only the Dead Know Brooklyn"

H. L. Mencken—a passage from "There are Parts for All in the *Totentanz*," in *Prejudices: Sixth Series*

The Hairy Ape, by Eugene O'Neill. The cage in question is the gorilla cage.

a. Frank O'Hara describes himself performing all these activities in his poem "The Day Lady Died."

b. The pictures of those mentioned and of others, including Johnny Groen (the owner), deck the walls of Stage-Door Johnny's in L. E. Sissman's poem "The West Forties: Morning, Noon and Night."

Apart from *42nd Street*, they are all mentioned in the Rodgers and Hart song "Manhattan" (though *My Fair Lady*—"a terrific show, they say"—only in the updated version, where it replaces the prediction that "our future babies/ we'll take to *Abie's/ Irish Rose*").

Manhattan Transfer by John Dos Passos—see the chapter "Great Lady on a White Horse"

a. Anthony Trollope in *North America* (The novel referred to in the question is *The American Senator*.)

b. Julian Symons—the opening lines of his poem "Central Park" (The entire poem is most readily accessible in *The Penguin Book of Light Verse.*)

c. G. K. Chesterton, according to "Meditation in Broadway" in his book *What I Saw in America*

"Bartleby, the Scrivener," by Herman Melville

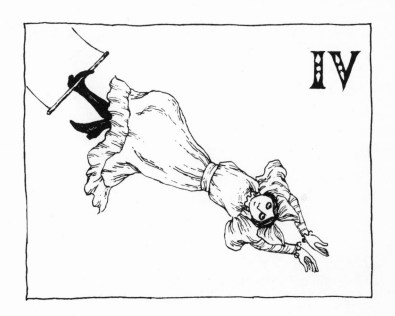

a. Alexander Pope—a pastiche of Chaucer from his "Imitations of the English Poets"

b. Rudyard Kipling. The poem from which these lines are taken, "Gertrude's Prayer," is the epigraph and also a source of contention in his story of rivalry and forgery, "Dayspring Mishandled" (in the collection *Limits and Renewals*).

2

They were all winners of the Nobel Prize for literature, in 1908, 1910, 1917, 1944, and 1953, respectively. Heyse and Eucken were German, Pontoppidan and Jensen were Danish, and Churchill was Churchill.

a. A travel book by D. H. Lawrence

b. A collection of stories by Ben Hecht

c. A collection of humorous pieces by Robert Benchley

The imaginary village in *Under Milk Wood* by Dylan Thomas. The name is "bugger all" spelled backward.

They all won the Pulitzer Prize for fiction. The authors and dates in question were Edna Ferber (1925), Julia Peterkin (1929), Josephine Johnson (1935), Booth Tarkington (1922), and Ernest Hemingway (1953).

a. The medieval philosopher and man of science Roger Bacon

b. St. Thomas Aquinas

c. St. Thomas Aquinas

Sexual Behavior in the Human Male by Alfred Kinsey and others

They all held the position of Poet Laureate—Whitehead from 1757 to 1785, Pye from 1790 to 1813, Austin from 1896 to 1913.

a. The men poets in the "thin anthology" described by Kingsley Amis in his poem "A Bookshop Idyll"

b. The women poets in the same anthology

Logan Pearsall Smith in "Afterthoughts," from *All Trivia*

a. A novel by Somerset Maugham (1925)

b. A novel by James Gibbons Huneker (1920) "The painted veil that men call life" is a phrase in a poem by Shelley.

They are tourists in the poem called "Tourists" by Howard Moss

a. A historical survey by V. L. Parrington

b. A short story by Irwin Shaw

a. George Bernard Shaw

b. T. S. Eliot (He subsequently married Valerie Fletcher.)

c. W. B. Yeats

Both titles come from poems by Andrew Marvell—from "To His Coy Mistress" and "Bermudas," respectively

Charles Bovary—she was Madame Bovary

a. Stephen Dedalus in *The Portrait of the Artist as a Young Man* (it has been suggested that the name is a child's attempt to say "Auntie").

b. Persse O'Reilly (or perhaps the dreamer) in "The Ballad of Persse O'Reilly" in *Finnegans Wake* was "fafafather of all schemes for to bother us." Apart from those mentioned they included "seven dry Sundays a week," "open-air love," and "religion's reform."

c. "Billy Walsh," that is to say William Walsh, the Archbishop of Dublin at the time—according to James Joyce in his poem "Gas from a Burner"

The authors are all primarily known as novelists

a. George Eliot

b. Norman Mailer

c. John Updike

d. Daniel Defoe

e. Graham Greene (his first book, published in 1925, while he was still at Oxford)

a. Samuel Goldwyn, reputedly after commissioning Maurice Maeterlinck to write a screenplay based on his most recent book, without realizing that it was *The Life of Bee*

b. According to the clerihew by Nicolas Bentley,
> *Cecil B. De Mille,*
> *Much against his will,*
> *Was persuaded to keep Moses*
> *Out of the Wars of the Roses*

Nicolas Bentley, best known as an illustrator, was the son of Edmund Clerihew Bentley, who invented the clerihew as a verse form

c. The authorized biography of the Hollywood mogul Carl Laemmle was written by Drinkwater, whose other major venture into the field of American biography was a verse play based on the life of Abraham Lincoln. According to a rhyme current in the 1920s,
> *Uncle Carl Laemmle*
> *Has a very large family*

a. A short play by Chekhov

b. A novel by J. M. Barrie

c. A novel by Turgenev

VI

FOOD

AND DRINK

Ben Jonson

2

a. Mr. Woodhouse, the heroine's father, in *Emma* by Jane Austen

b. The mock-medieval ballad by the Victorian light verse writer C. S. Calverley, which has the repeated refrain *Butter and eggs and a pound of cheese*

c. The curate's egg—the curate is addressing the bishop in a cartoon by George Du Maurier

d. In Thackeray's skit on Goethe, "The Sorrows of Werther," Charlotte, when she saw Werther's body borne before her on a shutter,

> Like a well-conducted person,
> Went on cutting bread and butter.

All three comments are to be found in Flaubert's *Dictionary of Received Ideas*.

a. John Keats

b. Dr. Johnson, complaining to Mrs. Thrale

In the chapter entitled "An Aged and a Great Wine" in George Meredith's novel *The Egoist*

Chum Frink is the local newspaper bard of Zenith, the midwestern city in which Sinclair Lewis's novel *Babbitt* is set.

King Mithridates in A. E. Housman's poem "Terence, This is Stupid Stuff"

Heartburn by Nora Ephron

Becky Sharp in Thackeray's *Vanity Fair*. ("Mr. S ———" is Mr. Sedley, and "R———" is of course for Rebecca.)

Sydney Smith, "Receipt for Making a Salad"
Serenely full, the epicure would say,
Fate cannot harm me, I have dined today.

Solution to the
First Crossword

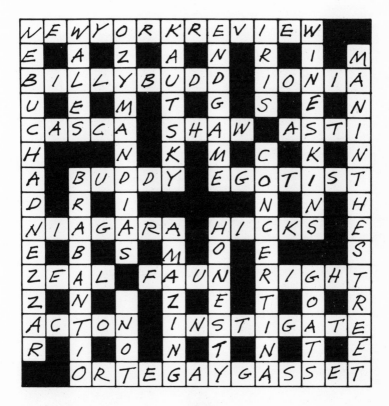

The crossword solution grid reads:

N	E	W	Y	O	R	K	R	E	V	I	E	W
E		A		Z		A		N		R	I	
B	I	L	L	Y	B	U	D	D		I	O	N	I	A
U		E		M		T		G		S	É		N
C	A	S	C	A		S	H	A	W		A	S	T	I

Notes

11a. In *Julius Caesar*; 12a. Lawrence of Arabia enlisted as Aircraftsman Shaw; 15a. "Can you spare a dime?"; 17a. Anagram of "Ra" and "again"; 19a. Edward Hicks, *The Peacable Kingdom*; 20a. Zeal-of-the-land Busy in Ben Jonson's *Bartholomew Fair*; 21a. Hawthorne, *The Marble Faun*

1d. A painting by Blake; 2d. The Welsh for "Wales"; 3d. Shelley's "Ozymandias"; 6d. Iris Murdoch; 15d. *Othello*; 18d. Meredith's novel *The Amazing Marriage*; 19d. *Othello*; 23d. *Othello*; 24a. Bernard Shaw's novel *The Irrational Knot*

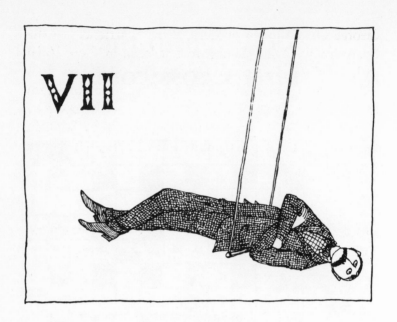

a. Johann Wolfgang Goethe, "A song over the unconfidence toward myself." Goethe wrote a number of early poems in English.

b. Rainer Maria Rilke, the first poem in the sequence "Les Roses." Rilke wrote a considerable number of poems in French.

"The trivial skirmish fought near Marathon"—according to Robert Graves in his poem "The Persian Version"

Provence. All the others have been offered homage— by Daniel Fuchs in his novel *Homage to Blenholt*; by

George Orwell in his account of his experiences in the Spanish Civil War, *Homage to Catalonia*; by Gore Vidal in his collection of essays *Homage to Daniel Shays*. It is a distinction they share with John Dryden (a collection of essays by T. S. Eliot), Sextus Propertius (the poem by Ezra Pound), the British Museum (a poem by William Empson) . . . Readers are invited to complete their own list.

Ernest Dowson, the 1890s poet, according to Ezra Pound in *Hugh Selwyn Mauberley*

Kim's full name was Kimball O'Hara—O'Hara as in Scarlett O'Hara. The phrase "gone with the wind" comes from Ernest Dowson's poem "Non Sum Qualis Eram," also known as "Cynara."

Edgar Allan Poe (". . . with his raven, like Barnaby Rudge"), according to James Russell Lowell in his poem *A Fable for Critics*

a. Winston Churchill in *My Early Life*

b. Adolf Hitler in *Mein Kampf*

King Leopold II of the Belgians, according to Vachel Lindsay in his poem "The Congo"—a reference to atrocities committed during the period when Leopold ruled the Belgian Congo (the present-day Zaire) as his personal fiefdom

a. Two novels by John P. Marquand have been telescoped together—*Yours Sincerely, Willis Wade* and *Women and Thomas Harrow.*

b. *Kingsblood Royal* is a novel by Sinclair Lewis; *Youngblood Hawke* is a novel by Herman Wouk.

c. *The Rise of Silas Lapham* is a novel by William Dean Howells; *The Rise of David Levinsky* is a novel by Abraham Cahan.

The original of Waring, who "gave us all the slip" in Robert Browning's poem "Waring," was Browning's friend Alfred Domett. In reality he went to New Zealand and became prime minister of that country before returning to England.

VIII

a. Peter Quilpe is a character in *The Cocktail Party*, by T. S. Eliot.

b. Peter Quint is the former valet in *The Turn of the Screw* by Henry James.

c. Peter Quince is the stage-manager of "Pyramus and Thisbe" in *A Midsummer Night's Dream*. There is also a poem by Wallace Stevens called "Peter Quince at the Clavier," although it is not altogether clear what part Peter Quince plays in it.

a. Arthur Koestler, while working as a journalist in Germany, wrote an encyclopaedia of sex under the pseudonym "A. Cosler." He was sentenced to death while a prisoner of the Fascists during the Spanish Civil War, but released through British intervention.

b. The French writer Robert Brasillach was coauthor with Maurice Bardèche of a history of the cinema. After World War II he was sentenced to death for his pro-Nazi activities and executed.

c. Sir Walter Raleigh wrote *The History of the World* while a prisoner in the Tower of London. He was subsequently released and undertook the second of his two expeditions to Guiana, but on his return he was charged with treason, convicted, and executed.

a. Utopia, in the book of that name by Sir Thomas More

b. Lilliput in *Gulliver's Travels*

c. Ruritania in *The Prisoner of Zenda* by Anthony Hope

a. Christopher Smart said it of Thomas Gray

b. Dr. Johnson said it of Christopher Smart

5

In a prominent bar in Secaucus one day
Rose a lady in skunk with a topheavy sway...

For the rest of what happened, see the poem "In a prominent bar in Secaucus" by X. J. Kennedy.

6

a. A play by Christopher Fry

b. The masochistic classic by Count Leopold von Sacher-Masoch

c. A musical with music by Kurt Weill, lyrics by Ogden Nash, and book by Nash and S. J. Perelman

They are all publishers. Reynal and Hitchcock and Boni and Liveright were American publishers. The English publishers Richard Bentley and Henry Colburn joined forces in 1830. Chapman and Hall, also founded in London in 1830, published Dickens and many other Victorian authors; Evelyn Waugh's father, Arthur Waugh, was chairman in the early years of the present century. Faber and Gwyer was the house that later changed its name to Faber and Faber; its most celebrated director was T. S. Eliot.

Mark Twain in his essay "The Damned Human Race"

The Bible. The Breeches Bible was the name given to the translation published by English exiles in Geneva in 1560, so called because it describes Adam and Eve as sewing fig leaves together and making themselves breeches. The Vinegar Bible, published in Oxford in 1717, has a misprint that describes the Parable of the Vineyard in the Book of Luke as "The Parable of the Vinegar." James Moffat of the Union Theological Seminary published translations of the Bible into modern English during the 1920s. Miles Coverdale's translation, the first complete translation of the Bible into English, was published in 1535. The Geneva Bible is a more formal name for the Breeches Bible.

The opening sentence of the Book of Genesis, translated into Esperanto.

IX CRIMINAL RECORDS

a. In *The Maltese Falcon* by Dashiell Hammett, it turns out that Miles Archer (Sam Spade's partner) was killed by Brigid O'Shaughnessy. Two other, rather more obvious malefactors in the same story are Caspar Gutman and Joel Cairo.

b. Personville—pronounced "Poisonville"—is the setting of Dashiell Hammett's *Red Harvest*. We are never told the name of the investigator in the story—he is known simply as the Continental Op.

a. Edgar Allan Poe—"The Mystery of Marie Roget"

b. Theodore Dreiser—*An American Tragedy*

116

The Chinese Orange Mystery, The Spanish Cape Mystery, The Dutch Shoe Mystery, and *The Roman Hat Mystery* are all stories by Ellery Queen.

a. Rex Stout

b. Agatha Christie

c. Erle Stanley Gardner, writing as "A. A. Fair." (She has a partner, called Donald Lam.)

E. C. Bentley's *Trent's Last Case* deals with the murder of Sigsbee Manderson; G. K. Chesterton dedicated his novel about anarchists, *The Man Who was Thursday,* to Bentley; Marie Belloc Lowndes, the sister of Chesterton's associate Hilaire Belloc, wrote a novel based on the Jack the Ripper murders entitled *The Lodger.*

Apart from Eddie Mars, they are all characters created by Ed McBain. Kling, Hawes, and Meyer are detectives in his 87th Precinct series, Matthew Hope is a lawyer who plays the detective in another series by him. (And Eddie Mars, for the record, is a gangster in *The Big Sleep* by Raymond Chandler.)

The proposal in Latin was made by Dorothy L. Sayers's hero Lord Peter Wimsey and accepted by her heroine Harriet Vane.

a. An essay on detective stories by W. H. Auden

b. An essay attacking genteel detective stories by Raymond Chandler

c. An essay by Thomas De Quincey

d. A monograph by Sherlock Holmes

e. An essay by Edmund Wilson in praise of Sherlock Holmes—in marked contrast to his onslaught on the latter-day detective story in "Who Cares Who Killed Roger Ackroyd?"

Gervase Fen is a detective who appears in the stories of Edmund Crispin; Gideon Fell is a detective who appears in the stories of John Dickson Carr

The Woman in White by Wilkie Collins

The English painter Gwen John. Rodin, who was her lover, once employed Rilke as a secretary; her brother Augustus John painted portraits of Dylan Thomas and numerous other literary figures, including Thomas Hardy, Bernard Shaw, and T. E. Lawrence.

a. William Burroughs

b. Hart Crane—his last recorded words before committing suicide

c. Sherwood Anderson

119

3

They are all characters whose thoughts are recorded in *The Waves*, by Virginia Woolf, with the exception of Clarissa (though that is the first name of the heroine of *Mrs. Dalloway*).

4

a. Swinburne in "Nephelidia," a parody of himself

b. Swinburne in "The Higher Pantheism," a parody of Tennyson

5

According to Alexander Pope,
> *Nature, and Nature's laws, lay hid in night.*
> *God cried, "Let Newton be!," and all was light.*

According to J. C. Squire, in the 1920s,
> *It could not last. The Devil crying "Ho!*
> *Let Einstein be!," restored the status quo.*

6

Sir Isaac Newton's pet dog Diamond is said to have provoked this cry from his master after knocking over a candle that set fire to an accumulation of manuscripts

7

a. John Richard William Alexander Dwyer was footman to Justinian Stubbs, Esquire—from the parody of George Crabbe in *Rejected Addresses* by James and Horatio Smith (1812).

b. From the alliterative poem "An Austrian army, awfully arrayed," generally credited to Alaric A. Watts (1797–1864)

c. From the double dactyl by John Hollander, in the collection *Jiggery-Pokery*, edited by Anthony Hecht and John Hollander. The complete poem runs

> *Higgledy-piggledy,*
> *Benjamin Harrison,*
> *Twenty-third President*
> *Was, and as such*
>
> *Served between Clevelands, and*
> *Save for this trivial*
> *Idiosyncrasy,*
> *Didn't do much.*

An account of Tolstoy in *Reminiscences of Tolstoy* by Maxim Gorky

D. H. Lawrence. His friend S. S. Koteliansky was nick-named "Kot"; a poem denouncing Bibbles ("You miserable little bitch of love-tricks") appears in the collection *Birds, Beasts and Flowers*.

a. A novel by Alexander Dumas père

b. A screenplay by Raymond Chandler

c. A novel of the 1890s making fun of Oscar Wilde, by Robert Hichens

121

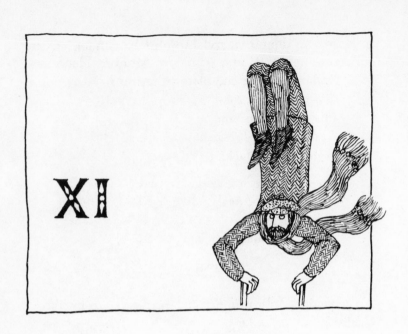

XI

John Keats, writing to his brother George, who had emigrated to America

a. She married Sidney Webb and became Beatrice Webb—or rather they became "the Webbs," celebrated British writers on politics and social history, leading members of the Fabian Society, and the object of H. G. Wells's satire in *The New Machiavelli*. Beatrice (who was also Malcolm Muggeridge's aunt) is very much not to be confused with Beatrix Potter, the author of *Peter Rabbit* and other well-loved children's books.

b. She became Mrs. Humphry Ward, the author of *Robert Elsmere* and other once highly esteemed novels, and a formidable presence on the late Victorian and early twentieth-century British literary scene. She was the niece of Matthew Arnold. A drawing by Max Beerbohm shows her as a small girl solemnly asking him why he cannot be always wholly serious. (There is a bonus point for correctly identifying *Mr. Humphry Ward*.)

c. She married Edward Robbins Wharton and wrote, among other things, *The House of Mirth*.

a. Montaigne in his essay "Apology for Raymond Sebond"

b. Tom and Jerry are the two chief characters who roister around town in Pierce Egan's *Life in London* (1821); by extension their names became a byword for uproarious goings-on in general.

c. She was the favorite cat, "demurest of the tabby kind," drowned in a tub of gold fishes and commemorated in an ode by Thomas Gray.

d. Mickey Mouse

e. Gordon Comstock, the hero or anti-hero of George Orwell's novel *Keep the Aspidistra Flying*

You must perform these operations "if you want in this world to advance"—according to a song in *Ruddigore* by Gilbert and Sullivan.

a. William Blake

b. William Maginn, early nineteenth-century Tory journalist and man of letters, renowned drinker, the original of "Captain Shandon" in Thackeray's *Pendennis*. "Maginnis" is the Latin genitive of Maginn.

c. John Gay, author of *The Beggar's Opera*

a. Thomas Mann
b. Sigmund Freud
c. Franz Kafka

Sigmund Freud

a. Froissart's *Chronicles* is the best known of the various works translated by Lord Berners, the second baron (1467–1533).

b. Gertrude Stein wrote the words for A *Wedding Bouquet*; the music was composed and the sets and costumes designed by Lord Berners, the fourteenth baron (1883–1950).

P. G. Wodehouse, "The Voice from the Past" (in the collection *Mulliner Nights*)

The apparition reported by John Aubrey in his *Miscellanies* as having been seen near Cirencester in 1670. "Being demanded, whether a good spirit or bad? it returned no answer, but disappeared with a curious perfume and a most melodious twang. Mr. W. Lillie believes it was a Fairie."

XII

ON STAGE

a. They were both actors—though Jean Baptiste Poquelin turned to play-writing and is better known under his pen name, Molière. Constant-Benoît Coquelin (1841–1909) was a celebrated French actor, best known for creating the part of Cyrano de Bergerac.

b. John Henry Brodribb was the real name of the Victorian actor Sir Henry Irving.

c. Like Garrick (whose family name was originally Garrigue), Olivier, as his name might suggest, is of Huguenot descent

d. Frances Kemble, a member of one of the most eminent of British theatrical families. She was married for a time to an American, wrote an account of her life on a Georgia plantation intended to influence British readers against slavery, and returned to America in her later years. Her aunt was Sarah Siddons; her grandson was Owen Wister, and the novel in question is *The Virginian*.

a. Samuel Johnson (There was also a musical called *Irene*, featuring the song "Alice Blue Gown," but that doesn't count.)

b. Samuel Taylor Coleridge

c. Henry James

3.

a. *The Resistible Rise of Arturo Ui*, by Brecht

b. *The Dog Beneath the Skin*, by Auden and Isherwood

c. The *Wasps*, by Aristophanes

d. They are both theatrical dogs—Nan in J. M. Barrie's *Peter Pan* and Sheba in William Inge's *Come Back, Little Sheba*.

4.

The Heiress (not to be confused with the stage adaptation of Henry James's *Washington Square*, also called *The Heiress*) is a comedy by John Burgoyne, a well-known playwright in his own time but better remembered today as the British General who surrendered at Saratoga in the War of Independence. He appears as a character in Bernard Shaw's play *The Devil's Disciple*.

5.

a. "Rossum's Universal Robots" in the play *R.U.R.* by Karel Capek

b. *The Adding Machine* by Elmer Rice

a. The lavatory, in the song "The Stately Homes of England" by Noël Coward

b. Elvira, the ghost in Noël Coward's play *Blithe Spirit*. Shelley's "Ode to the Skylark" opens "Hail to thee, blithe spirit!"; Elvira was also the name of Don Juan's wife.

c. In their "Last Will and Testament" in *Letters from Iceland*, W. H. Auden and Louis MacNeice include among their legacies "a place in the setting sun," which they bequeath to Noël Coward

a. The mid-Victorian editor of *Punch*, Tom Taylor, was also the author of *Our American Cousin*, the play that Lincoln was watching when he was assassinated.

b. Vladimir Mayakovsky; the play is *The Bedbug*

c. Ibsen; the play is *The Wild Duck*

The Spanish Armada is the absurd historical play by Sir Fretful Plagiary in Sheridan's comedy *The Critic*

a. Oscar Wilde, according to John Betjeman's poem "The Arrest of Oscar Wilde at the Cadogan Hotel"

b. "Speranza" was the pen name of Oscar Wilde's mother; "C.3.3."—his cell-number as a convict—was the pen name under which Wilde originally published "The Ballad of Reading Gaol."

a. John Hall married Susanna Shakespeare and Thomas Quiney married Judith Shakespeare; they were Shakespeare's two sons-in-law.

b. Freud was persuaded by Looney's book on the subject that Shakespeare's plays had actually been written by the Earl of Oxford.

c. "Robin Goodfellow" is an alternative name for Puck, the part played by Mickey Rooney in Max Reinhardt's movie version of *A Midsummer Night's Dream*.

XIII

♦

a. William Shakespeare and possibly Lewis Theobald. In the First Folio, the famous description of the dying Falstaff read "and a table of green fields." Theobald's emendation, put forward in the early eighteenth century, has been generally accepted.

b. John Milton and Richard Bentley. Bentley, though one of the greatest classical scholars England ever produced, perpetrated one of the most bizarre aberrations of English scholarship, his revision of *Paradise Lost* (1732), which was based on the assumption that Milton's text had been garbled by an incompetent amanuensis and poor editing. Probably his most notorious change was the last lines of the poem, "They hand in hand, with wandering steps and slow,/Through Eden took their solitary way," which he changed to "They hand in hand with social steps their way/Through Eden took with heavenly comfort cheer'd." "No light, but rather a transpicuous gloom" is his improved version of "No light, but rather darkness visible."

They are both portraits of Bertrand Russell, Sir Joshua in D. H. Lawrence's novel *Women in Love* and Mr. Apollinax in T. S. Eliot's poem "Mr. Apollinax"

a. William Cowper

b. Catullus

c. Robert Louis Stevenson. Vailima, which is in Samoa, was his last home.

d. Victor Hugo, who lived there for eighteen years as an exile from the Second Empire

e. Voltaire

Brooches—the other items are to be found, as listed, on Belinda's dressing-table in Pope's *Rape of the Lock*.

a. Sherwood Anderson

b. Gunnar Myrdal (subsequently known as *Race: An American Dilemma*)

c. Erskine Caldwell. This work of reportage also had photographs taken by his former wife, Margaret Bourke-White.

a. On the coast of Coromandel, in Edward Lear's poem about Coromandel

b. The young lady of Smyrna, in Edward Lear's limerick

c. Edward Lear, in the poem he wrote about himself, "By Way of a Preface" ("How pleasant to know Mr. Lear!").

The plot of *The Turn of the Screw* was suggested to Henry James by a story he heard from the then Archbishop of Canterbury, E. W. Benson. One of Benson's sons, A. C. Benson, wrote the words of "Land of Hope and Glory" (set to music by Elgar, and for a time accorded the status of something very like a second British National Anthem). Another son, E. F. Benson, wrote numerous novels, including the "Lucia" series; a third son, R. H. Benson, became a Roman Catholic priest and received Ronald Firbank into the Church.

Uncle Ponderevo, the patent medicine king in H. G. Wells's novel *Tono-Bungay*. Wells is said to have based part of this scene on what he saw and heard at the deathbed of a very different character, the novelist George Gissing.

a. "Somerville and Ross" (Edith Oenone Somerville and Violet Martin), who are best known as the authors of *Some Experiences of an Irish R.M.*—but the novel *The Real Charlotte* is their masterpiece

b. A play by James Thurber and Elliot Nugent

c. *The Custom of the Country* is the title of a novel by Edith Wharton; but long before that it was the title of a play, written around 1620, by John Fletcher and Philip Massinger.

a.   *The cat, the rat, and Lovell the dog*
       Rule all England under the hog.

The hog was Richard III; Catesby the cat, Ratcliffe the rat, and Lovell the dog were three of his principal henchmen. This anonymous rhyme of the period is probably best known to modern audiences for having been used by Laurence Olivier in his movie version of *Richard III*.

b.   *I am his Highness' dog at Kew;*
       Pray tell me, sir, whose dog are you?

Lines written by Alexander Pope and inscribed on the collar of a dog belonging to Frederick, Prince of Wales. They make a decidedly satirical point, if you think about it.

Solution to the
Second Crossword

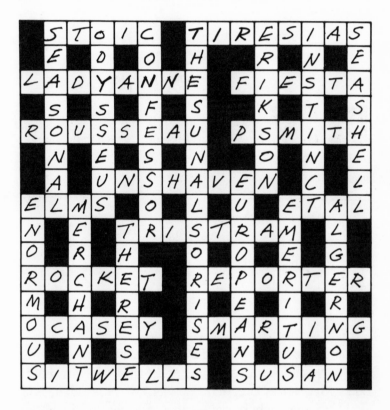

The crossword grid reads:

S	T	O	I	C		T	I	R	E	S	I	A	S
E		D		O		H		R		N			E
L	A	D	Y	A	N	N	E		F	I	E	S	T	A
S		S		F		S			K		T		S
R	O	U	S	S	E	A	U		P	S	M	I	T	H
N		E		S		N			O		N		E
A		U	N	S	H	A	V	E	N		C		L
E	L	M	S		O		L		U		E	T	A	L
N		E		T	R	I	S	T	R	A	M		L
O		R		H		S		O		O	E		G
R	O	C	K	E	T		R	E	P	O	R	T	E	R
M		H		R			I		E		I		R
O		C	A	S	E	Y		S	M	A	R	T	I	N	G
U		N		S			E		N		U		O
S	I	T	W	E	L	L	S		S	U	S	A	N

Notes

1a. *The Stoic* by Dreiser; 8a. *Richard III*; 9a. *Fiesta* is the title of the British edition; 14a. *Desire Under the Elms*; 18a. Tristram and Isolde, *Tristram Shandy*; 24a. in *Lady Susan*

1d. James Thomson, *The Seasons*; 3d. Edward the Confessor; 5d. *Young Man Luther, Gandhi's Truth*; 13d. *The Europeans* by Henry James; 14d. E. E. Cummings; 15d. *The Merchant's Tale* by Chaucer, *The Merchant of Venice*; 17d. Algernon Sidney, Algernon Charles Swinburne; 18d. *Thérèse Raquin* by Zola, *Thérèse Desqueyroux* by Mauriac

A composite figure, created by the notoriously right-wing poet Roy Campbell, consisting of the then left-wing poets Louis MacNeice, Stephen Spender, W. H. Auden, and C. Day Lewis, whose names were frequently linked together during the 1930s

a. George Meredith—the novel is *The Tragic Comedians*

b. A satirical account of fashionable life in the 1930s by Cyril Connolly

c. They are all buried in Highgate Cemetery, London.

Frank Sullivan's Cliché Expert, in "The Cliché Expert Testifies on Love" (from Sullivan's collection *A Pearl in Every Oyster*, though it has also appeared in several anthologies)

There was no cheap red wine among the cargoes being carried by a quinquireme, a galleon, and a steamer in John Masefield's poem "Cargoes"—although there was some sweet white wine, and all the other items listed in the question

a. Michelangelo

b. John Addington Symonds (Fusato was a gondolier)

c. Marcel Proust

a. Voltaire's rebuke to Congreve, who when he visited him told him that he preferred to be thought of as a gentleman rather than a writer

b. Dr. Johnson, replying to the lady who asked him why he had incorrectly defined the word "pastern" in his Dictionary as "the knee of a cow."

c. Henry James, on being asked by a young man what John Cross felt when George Eliot died only seven months after he had married her

Generally attributed to Humbert Wolfe, this is one of

several rhymed retorts to W. N. Ewer's lines
> *How odd*
> *Of God*
> *To choose*
> *The Jews.*

They are all reputed to be the coinages of the early twentieth-century San Francisco-born cartoonist Thomas Aloysius Dorgan, or "Tad."

Thomas de Quincey, in *Confessions of an English Opium-Eater*

a. Aubrey Beardsley

b. James Thurber

c. Stevie Smith

Answers to the Pictorial Quiz

Coleridge's *The Rime of the Ancient Mariner*—Gustave Doré

Poe's *The Raven*—Edouard Manet

Melville's *Moby Dick*—Rockwell Kent

George MacDonald's *At The Back of the North Wind*—
Arthur Hughes

Lewis Carroll's *The Hunting of the Snark*—Henry Holiday

Pope's *The Rape of the Lock*—Aubrey Beardsley

Wilhelm Busch's *Max and Moritz*—Wilhelm Busch

Dickens's *Dombey and Son* —H. K. Browne ("Phiz")

James's *What Maisie Knew*—Edward Gorey

XV

BRUSH AND PALETTE

Sir Joshua Reynolds, as described in Oliver Goldsmith's poem "Retaliation"

a. A play by Pablo Picasso

b. The poem of that name by Wallace Stevens was partly inspired by Picasso, though Stevens said he didn't have any one painting in mind, and has in its turn inspired a series of pictures by David Hockney.

3

a. Dante Gabriel Rossetti

b. Degas

c. A character based on Whistler in George du Maurier's novel *Trilby*. When the novel first appeared in serial form Whistler took legal advice and threatened the author with violence; the portrayal was subsequently toned down.

Martin Droeshout engraved (not very brilliantly) the portrait of Shakespeare on the title page of the First Folio; Giulio Romano is the only Italian Old Master mentioned in Shakespeare's plays (in *The Winter's Tale*)

Jackson Pollock, according to Phyllis McGinley in "A Spectator's Guide to Contemporary Art"

a. *Daniel Deronda* by George Eliot

b. *To the Lighthouse* by Virginia Woolf

c. *The Doctor's Dilemma* by Bernard Shaw

d. The "Music of Time" sequence by Anthony Powell

e. *The Moon and Sixpence* by Somerset Maugham

Leonardo Da Vinci describing the design for The Last Supper in one of his notebooks

a. A story by Henry James

b. A story by J. D. Salinger

c. A story by Aldous Huxley

a. They are memoirs by celebrated writers on art—Bernard Berenson, John Ruskin, and Kenneth Clark.

b. They are all memoirs by celebrated painters—George Grosz, Paul Gauguin, and Walter Sickert.

Sir Joshua Reynolds, according to an epigram by William Blake

XVI

In Joyce's *Ulysses*, Stephen Dedalus, who has recently returned to Dublin from Paris, reminds himself that he owes some money to G. W. Russell—and since Russell was better known as the writer "A. E.", and since Joyce was Joyce, his reminder takes the form "A.E.I.O.U." Black, white, red, green, and blue are the colors of the respective vowels in Rimbaud's poem *Les Voyelles*.

a. It is a poem by Randall Jarrell.

b. It is a novel by William Gass.

3

The diary (a selection from it has been published under the title *Chips*) was kept by Henry Channon, an American expatriate who became a British member of parliament. The haggard young man he describes was Jean Cocteau; his other neighbor at table was Marcel Proust.

a. An argument that proved he was the Pope

b. A banker's clerk descending from a bus

c. A rattlesnake that questioned him in Greek

For further elucidation, see the poem by Lewis Carroll—"He thought he saw a banker's clerk..." in which all three episodes occur. (It originally appeared in his story *Sylvie and Bruno*.)

"The History of England by a partial, prejudiced and ignorant historian" is a skit written by Jane Austen when she was fifteen.

a. The Book of Ecclesiastes

b. Gogol's story *The Nose*

c. Mario Praz's study of nineteenth-century romanticism *The Romantic Agony*

Dr. Fell—and he couldn't say why. Thomas Brown (1663–1704) wrote a famous quatrain about the head of his Oxford college, John Fell, inspired by an epigram by Martial:

> *I do not love thee, Dr. Fell,*
> *The reason why I cannot tell;*
> *But this I know, and know full well,*
> *I do not love thee, Dr. Fell.*

There is a play by Clifford Odets called *Paradise Lost* and a study of the American automobile industry by Emma Rothschild called *Paradise Lost*—and further research may well reveal other works called *Paradise Lost*.

They are all fictional characters based on Huey Long, and they can be found in the following novels: Buzz Windrip in *It Can't Happen Here*, by Sinclair Lewis; Chuck Crawford in *Number One*, by John Dos Passos; Willie Stark in *All the King's Men*, by Robert Penn Warren.

A slug-horn is a variant on the Gaelic word "slogan," meaning a battle-cry, which was incorrectly used by Thomas Chatterton in his eighteenth-century "medieval" forgeries, the Rowley poems, and borrowed from Chatterton by Browning, who was under the impression that it was the name for a kind of horn.

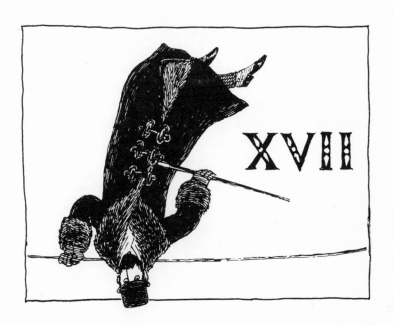

"Hans Breitmann gife a barty"—the opening line of C. G. Leland's poem "Hans Breitmann's Party"

All three poems can be found in Aldous Huxley's novel *Antic Hay*.

According to the gangsterish Wolfsheim, in *The Great Gatsby*, Jay Gatsby was an "Oggsford" man

It is an example of colloquial English from José de Fonsecca's *New Guide to Portuguese and English*, the unintentionally bizarre nineteenth-century Portuguese handbook popularized in America by Mark Twain and better known as *English as She Is Spoke.*

a. Ruth McKenney (her sister Eileen, incidentally, was married to Nathanael West)

b. Jerome Weidman

c. Daphne du Maurier

a. It was the motto of the *Edinburgh Review* (founded in 1802 by Francis Jeffrey and others).

b. The source of the name of the magazine *Hound and Horn*, edited between 1927 and 1934 by Lincoln Kirstein, R. P. Blackmur, and others

The missing names are Hollywood, Palm Springs, Las Vegas, and Beverly Hills; the couplets come from John Berryman's poem "American Lights, Seen from Off Abroad."

They all edited magazines (different magazines) called the *Dial*—Margaret Fuller in the 1840s, Moncure Conway in the 1860s, Scofield Thayer in the 1920s.

a. The English historian G. M. Trevelyan wrote extensively about the Italian Risorgimento; the hero of Trollope's novel *He Knew He Was Right* is called Louis Trevelyan.

b. Jake Barnes, the hero of Hemingway's novel *The Sun Also Rises*, is a newspaperman who has been emasculated by a war wound; the Reverend William Barnes wrote poems in Dorsetshire dialect much admired by Thomas Hardy and many others.

c. The cultured and idealistic sisters are Helen and Margaret Schlegel in E. M. Forster's novel *Howards End*; the literary brothers were August Wilhelm and Friedrich von Schlegel.

Hegel, according to Hans Breitmann in C. G. Leland's poem "Breitmann in Politics"

> *Ash der Hegel say of his system—dat only von mans knew*
>
> *Vot der tyfel id meant—und he couldn't tell—und der Jean Paul Richter, too,*
>
> *Who said, "Gott knows I meant somedings vhen foorst dis buch I writ,*
>
> *Boot Gott only wise vot das buch mean now—for I hafe fergotten it."*

XVIII

CHILDREN'S HOUR

The Wizard of Oz in the story of that name by L. Frank Baum

Babar the Elephant, subsequently King Babar, in the stories by Jean and Laurent de Brunhoff

a. Peter Rabbit in *The Tale of Peter Rabbit* by Beatrix Potter

b. Rat and Mole in *The Wind in the Willows* by Kenneth Grahame

Jo March in *Little Women* by Louisa May Alcott

The mayor in "The Pied Piper of Hamelin," by Robert Browning

a. E. B. White in *Charlotte's Web*

b. Hergé in the Tintin stories

c. E. Nesbit in a series of books, beginning with *The Story of the Treasure-Seekers*

a. Dr. Seuss

b. Felix Salten, the author of *Bambi*

c. On the death of his uncles he becomes little Lord Fauntleroy, in the story of that name by Frances Hodgson Burnett

a. Maurice Sendak

b. Wanda Gag

c. Norton Juster

a. *The Little Prince* by Antoine de Saint-Exupéry

b. Arthur Ransome, author of the "Swallows and Amazons" series

The twelve-year-old Penrod Schofield, in *Penrod* by Booth Tarkington. The remark was made by his great-aunt.

XIX

a. John Ruskin

b. Mary McCarthy

c. Tennessee Williams

Ezra Pound's nickname for the Imagist movement in poetry after he felt it had succumbed to the influence of Amy Lowell

a. Murdstone and Grinby, the firm in which Mr. Murdstone is a partner in *David Copperfield*

b. Liddell and Scott, the standard Greek lexicon, first published in 1843. (Liddell's other claim to fame is that his daughter was the original of Alice in Wonderland.)

c. Thomas Boileau and Pierre Narcejac, French authors who have collaborated on numerous mystery stories

d. Harrigan and Hart, a celebrated American vaudeville team in the late nineteenth century. Edward Harrigan (1845–1911) also wrote a large number of sketches and plays, appearing in all of them himself.

e. Howard Lindsay and Russell Crouse collaborated on the dramatization of *Life with Father* and other subsequent ventures on Broadway.

They are all the titles of poems by John Ashbery.

a. Sir Rufus Israels is a minor character in Proust's *A la recherche du temps perdu*

b. The character of Swann in the same novel is partly based on Charles Ephrussi and Charles Haas.

a. Macondo is the imaginary village in which Gabriel García Márquez set *A Hundred Years of Solitude*.

b. Costaguana is the imaginary country in which Joseph Conrad set *Nostromo*.

William Strachey's account of a shipwreck in Bermuda in 1609 is generally thought to have influenced Shakespeare in writing *The Tempest*. Strachey was an ancestor of, among other notable figures, John Strachey, whose book *The Coming Struggle for Power* was a widely read more-or-less Marxist text of the 1920s; Lytton Strachey, whose first book (published in 1912) was *Landmarks in French Literature*; and Lytton's brother James, the principal English translator of the collected works of Freud.

Richard Strauss's opera *Die schweigsame Frau* is based on Ben Jonson's play *Epicene, or the Silent Woman*. It was banned in Nazi Germany from 1935 onward because the author of the libretto, Stefan Zweig, was Jewish.

The exchange described takes place between Mrs. Lightfoot Lee and Senator Silas P. Ratcliffe, the two main characters in Henry Adams's novel *Democracy*.

a. Macheath in John Gay's *The Beggar's Opera*—see the song "Were I laid on Greenland's coast."

b. Macheath in Brecht's *Threepenny Opera*—see the song "Mack the Knife." (In the English translation, the body is described as "oozing life.")

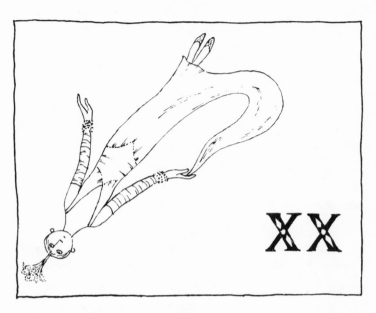

The Canterbury Tales. Harry Bailly is the name of the Host of the Tabard Inn who proposes that the pilgrims lighten the journey by telling one another stories.

Tolstoy's *Resurrection* (filmed by Samuel Goldwyn)

a. Anna Seward (1747–1809), known as the "Swan of Lichfield," was a poet, a friend of Erasmus Darwin and his circle, and one of Boswell's most important informants about the early life of Dr. Johnson (her grandfather had been one of Johnson's teachers). Anna Sewell was the author of *Black Beauty* (1877), the children's classic about the life of a horse.

b. Senlin is the speaker in Conrad Aiken's poem "Morning Song of Senlin." Senlac is a site near Hastings where

William the Conqueror defeated the English forces under Harold in 1066; the Battle of Hastings was formerly also referred to as the Battle of Senlac.

c. Richard Cory is the perfect gentleman with a suicidal impulse in the poem named after him by Edward Arlington Robinson. William Johnson Cory (1832–1892) is best known for his translation of a Greek epigram—"They told me Heraclitus, they told me you were dead"; he was a master at the English private school, Eton, and also wrote the "Eton Boating Song."

d. Julian English is the hero of John O'Hara's novel *Appointment in Samarra*. "William Irish" was the pen name adopted by Cornell Woolrich for many of his detective stories.

e. Potterism is (or was) a synonym for commercialism and cheap journalism—from the novel of that name by Rose Macaulay. One-upmanship is a system for getting the better of other people devised—along with Lifemanship and Gamesmanship—by Stephen Potter.

> *I don't like the family Stein:*
> *There is Gert, there is Ep, there is Ein.*
> *Gert's writings are bunk,*
> *Ep's statues are junk,*
> *And no one can understand Ein.*

Anon.

a. Bishop Berkeley—George Berkeley, Bishop of Cloyne. (The poem contains the line "Westward the course of empire takes its way.")

b. They were both bishops (Dr. Proudie in Trollope's *Barchester Towers*; Talleyrand was consecrated bishop of Autun as a young man).

c. Sylvester Blougram in the poem by Robert Browning, "Bishop Blougram's Apology."

Who would not give all else for two p
Ennyworth only of beautiful soup?

From the song "Beautiful Soup" in *Alice in Wonderland.*

The speaker who doesn't know where she is running to is Flora Finching, addressing Arthur Clennam (her former lover, who has just returned to England from China after many years) in *Little Dorrit* by Charles Dickens.

The Web and the Rock is a novel (by Thomas Wolfe); all the others are works of literary or literary-cum-philosophical criticism—*The Hedgehog and the Fox* by Isaiah Berlin; *The Lion and the Fox* by Wyndham Lewis; *The Lion and the Honeycomb* by R. P. Blackmur; and *The Mirror and the Lamp* by M. H. Abrams

a. Ford Madox Ford
b. George Santayana
c. Wyndham Lewis

d. Osbert Sitwell

e. Sean O'Casey

Jean Webster, the author of *Daddy-Long-legs*, was the grandniece of Mark Twain.

XXI
SHAKESPEARE
AND
CO.

a. Rudyard Kipling, "Proofs of Holy Writ"

b. Anthony Burgess, *Nothing Like the Sun*

c. Bernard Shaw, *Shakes v. Shav* (where Shakes is, needless to say, knocked out by Shav)

At the Theatre Royal, Drury Lane, in Thomas Hood's poem "A Nocturnal Sketch"

> *Even is come; and from the dark park, hark,*
> *The signal of the setting sun—one gun!*
> *And six is sounding from the chime, prime time*
> *To go and see the Drury-Lane Dane slain,*
> *Or hear Othello's jealous doubt spout out,*
> *Or Macbeth raving at that shade-made blade,*
> *Denying to his frantic clutch, much touch...*

159

Walt Whitman (in *Poet-Lore*)

a. They are both the setting of stories with Shakespearean parallels—"Lady Macbeth of the Mtsensk District" by Nikolai Leskov, and "A Lear of the Steppes" by Turgenev

b. Catherine the Great of Russia

W. S. Gilbert (of Gilbert and Sullivan) thought up these lines and successfully palmed them off as a quotation by Shakespeare on the fellow-members of his London club.

They both acted the part of Hamlet (Wopsle in *Great Expectations* by Dickens).

Horace Walpole

Mary Lamb—the author, in collaboration with her brother Charles, of *Tales from Shakespear* (1807)

Cards of Identity, by Nigel Dennis; Blanche and Tray are two of the little dogs that King Lear, in his distraction, imagines barking at him.

There are strong indications in *Henry IV* that Falstaff was originally called Oldcastle, but that the name was changed because of objections that the historical Sir John Oldcastle, a leader of the Lollards or religious reformers who was executed during the reign of Henry V, was in fact a pious man and a martyr.

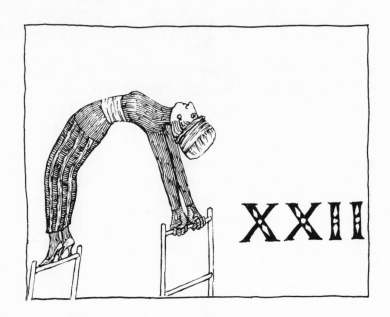

Behold a proof of Irish sense,
Here Irish wit is seen!
When nothing's left that's worth defence,
They build a magazine.

An epigram on the building of a new magazine for arms and gunpowder in Dublin by Jonathan Swift (though his authorship has been queried by some scholars)

a. The words of "America the Beautiful"

b. The words of "America" ("My country, 'tis of thee . . ."), which he wrote while a student at Andover Theological Seminary in 1831

c. The words of "The Star-Spangled Banner," set to Smith's music by Francis Scott Key in 1814

a. Edmund Wilson, "The Muse in the Parking-Lot"

b. William Empson, "Your Teeth are Ivory Towers"

c. Richard Eberhart, "I Went to See Irving Babbitt"

The Chocolate Soldier is an operetta by Oscar Strauss based on Bernard Shaw's play *Arms and the Man*, which takes its title from the opening line of Dryden's translation of Virgil's *Aeneid* ("Arms, and the man I sing..."—*Arma virumque cano.*)

Randall Jarrell in his novel *Pictures from an Institution*

a. A couplet from Lewis Carroll's "Jabberwocky," translated into Latin:

> *One, two! one, two! and through and through*
> *His vorpal blade went snicker-snack...*

b. A couplet from Lewis Carroll's "Jabberwocky," translated into German:

> *"Oh frabjous day! Callooh, callay!"*
> *He chortled in his joy.*

a. Corporal Trim is a character in *Tristram Shandy* by Laurence Sterne.

b. "Captain Carpenter" is a poem by John Crowe Ransom.

c. "My Kinsman, Major Molineaux" is a story by Nathaniel Hawthorne.

d. Colonel Brandon marries Marianne Dashwood in Jane Austen's *Sense and Sensibility.*

e. General Aupick was Charles Baudelaire's stepfather—and a figure for whom the poet felt little if any affection.

a. The Village Blacksmith in the poem of that name by Longfellow

b. Casey in "Casey at the Bat" by Ernest Lawrence Thayer

c. The "wonderful one-hoss shay" in Oliver Wendell Holmes's poem "The Deacon's Masterpiece"

A pseudonym used by Honoré de Balzac in his early writings—"R'hoone" is an anagram of "Honoré"

The Mystery of Edwin Drood, by Charles Dickens—which was of course unfinished at the time of the author's death.

Solution to the
Third Crossword

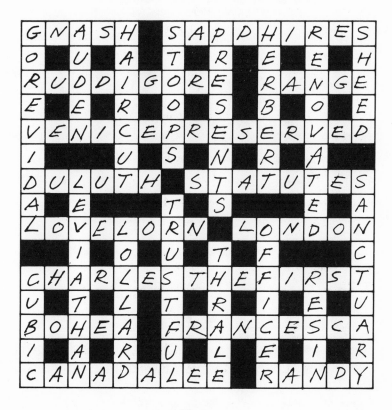

G	N	A	S	H		S	A	P	P	H	I	R	E	S
O		U		A		T		R		E		E		H
R	U	D	D	I	G	O	R	E		R	A	N	G	E
E		E		R		O		S		B		O		E
V	E	N	I	C	E	P	R	E	S	E	R	V	E	D
I		N		U		S		N		R		A		
D	U	L	U	T	H		S	T	A	T	U	T	E	S
A		E		T		S		S		E		E		A
L	O	V	E	L	O	R	N		L	O	N	D	O	N
		I		O		U		T		F				C
C	H	A	R	L	E	S	T	H	E	F	I	R	S	T
U		T		L		T		R		I		E		U
B	O	H	E	A		F	R	A	N	C	E	S	C	A
I		A		R		U		L		E		I		R
C	A	N	A	D	A	L	E	E		R	A	N	D	Y

Notes

1a. Gabriel Nash in *The Tragic Muse* by Henry James; 4a. T. S. Eliot, *Four Quartets*; 10a. The song "Home on the Range"; 11a. a play by Thomas Otway; 12a. On Lake Superior; 19a. *Martin Eden* by Jack London; 22a. Marvell's "Horatian Ode"; 25a. Paolo and Francesca

2d. In *Lions and Shadows* by Christopher Isherwood; 3d. Oliver Goldsmith, *She Stoops to Conquer* and "When lovely woman stoops to folly" in *The Vicar of Wakefield*; 6d. George Herbert, Zbigniew Herbert; 8d. Sheed and Ward; 15d. Temple Drake in *Sanctuary* by William Faulkner; 20d. *Officers and Gentlemen* by Evelyn Waugh; 21d. Dr. Johnson's friend Mrs. Thrale became Mrs. Piozzi by her second marriage

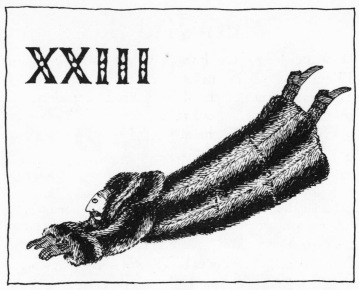

a. Theodore Roosevelt

b. Thomas Jefferson

c. Herbert Hoover

d. Dwight D. Eisenhower

e. John Quincy Adams (The *Oxford Companion to American Literature* says of the *Report on Weights and Measures* that "the subject is examined with the exactness of mathematical science, the sagacity of statesmanship, and the wisdom of philosophy.")

a. A biography of Calvin Coolidge by William Allen White

b. A play by Jerome Lawrence and Robert E. Lee based on the administration of Warren G. Harding

c. A play about Franklin D. Roosevelt by Dore Schary

3♦

These are the opening lines of Robert Frost's "For John F. Kennedy His Inauguration." At the Inauguration itself the strong wind and the light in his eyes made it impossible for Frost to read more than a few lines, after which he abandoned the effort and read his celebrated poem "The Gift Outright" instead.

4♦

The villainous Blofeld and the C.I.A. man Felix Leiter are both characters in the James Bond stories by Ian Fleming.

Garfield and Felix (who kept on walking in a once-popular movie series) are both cartoon cats.

Felix Unger and Oscar Madison are the "odd couple" in Neil Simon's play and subsequent movie and TV adaptations.

Felix Randall the farrier and Henry Purcell the composer are both the subject of poems by Gerard Manley Hopkins.

Felix Holt is a character in the novel of that name by George Eliot; Savonarola is one of the historical figures who plays an important role in her novel *Romola*.

Arthur M. Schlesinger, Jr. (who shares his name as well as his profession with his father). His first book, *Orestes Brownson*, was published in 1939; he won the Pulitzer Prize in 1946 for his historical study *The Age of Jackson*.

In Peyton Place—or rather, in *Return to Peyton Place*, where her novel *Samuel's Castle* lifts the lid off some local scandals

Bertrand Russell, who was unable to take up an appointment at the City College of New York after it had been objected that his teachings were immoral. His first wife's sister Mary was married to Bernard Berenson, and lived with him at I Tatti, near Florence; his brother married the novelist "Elizabeth" (Elizabeth Beauchamp), who had previously been married to Count von Arnim and written about her life with him in her first novel, *Elizabeth and Her German Garden*.

a. A thriller by Robert Ludlum

b. Another thriller—why not?—by Robert Ludlum

c. A historical study about America's entry into World War I by Barbara Tuchman

They are all incorrect. As the wife of Sir Harold Nicolson, Vita Sackville-West was Lady Nicolson (without the "Vita"). It should be Nathanael West, not Nathaniel. Although he was Cecil Day-Lewis in private life, the poet wrote under the name of C. Day Lewis, without a hyphen.

a. The Chinese poet Li Po

b. The short-story writer Saki, whose real name was Hector Hugh Munro, and who was killed while serving in the trenches in World War I

c. The Emperor Nero—the Latin is "Qualis artifex pereo"

Grateful acknowledgment is given for the following excerpts:

From "Your Teeth Are Ivory Towers" from *Collected Poems* by William Empson. Copyright 1949, © 1977 by William Empson. Reprinted by permission of Harcourt, Brace, Jovanovich, Inc., Chatto & Windus and the estate of the author.

From *The Poetry of Robert Frost* edited by Edward Connery Lathem. Copyright © 1961, 1962 by Robert Frost. Copyright © 1969 by Holt, Rinehart & Winston. Reprinted by permission of Henry Holt and Co., Inc.

From the "Benjamin Harrison" double dactyl by John Hollander. Copyright © 1966 Anthony Hecht and John Hollander. Reprinted by permission of Atheneum Publishers, Inc.

From "Tourists" from "A Swim Off the Rocks" (1976) in *New Selected Poems.* Copyright © 1985 Howard Moss. Reprinted by permission of Atheneum Publishers, Inc.

From "The Muse in the Parking Lot" from *Night Thoughts* by Edmund Wilson. Copyright 1953, © 1961 by Edmund Wilson. Reprinted by permission of Farrar, Straus, and Giroux, Inc.

From "Invitation to Miss Marianne Moore" from *Collected Poems* by Elizabeth Bishop. Copyright 1948, copyright renewed © 1976 by Elizabeth Bishop. Reprinted by permission of Farrar, Straus, and Giroux, Inc.

From "American Lights, Seen from Off Abroad" from *Short Poems* by John Berryman. Copyright 1953, © 1961 by John Berryman. Reprinted by permission of Farrar, Straus, and Giroux, Inc.

From "Gas from a Burner" from *The Portable James Joyce.* Copyright © 1964, 1967 by the Estate of James Joyce. Reprinted by permission of the Society of Authors as the literary representatives of the Estate of James Joyce and Viking Penguin, Inc.

From *Antic Hay* by Aldous Huxley. Copyright 1923 by Aldous Huxley; copyright renewed 1951 by Aldous Huxley. Reprinted by permission of Harper & Row Publishers, Inc., and Mrs. Laura Huxley.

From "Harvard" from *Notebook* by Robert Lowell. Copyright © 1967, 1968, 1969, by Robert Lowell. Reprinted by permission of Farrar, Straus, and Giroux, Inc., and Faber and Faber Ltd.